Luan Ferr

Arcturian Oracle
The Dance of Chaos

Original Title: Oráculo Arcturiano - A Dança Do Caos
Copyright © 2023 by Luan Ferr
2nd Edition © 2024 by Luan Ferr
All rights reserved by Booklas.com
This book is intended for personal and spiritual development. The information and practices described herein are based on studies, traditional knowledge, and the experiences of authors and specialists in this field. This content does not substitute medical advice or conventional therapies, serving only as a complementary resource for well-being and personal growth.

Editor
Luiz Antonio dos Santos
Translator
Ethan Harper
Text Revision
Gabriel Monteiro
Beatriz Cardoso
João Pereira
Graphic Design and Layout
Clara Martins
Cover
Studio Booklas / Lucas Nogueira

Content Classification:
Spirituality / Personal Development / Mysticism
Data Cataloging:
I. Monteiro, Gabriel. II. Title.
Cutter: 09-4267
DDC (Dewey Decimal Classification): 291.4 (Spirituality and Mysticism)
UDC (Universal Decimal Classification): 159.9 (Psychology and Spiritual Development)

All rights reserved by Booklas Publishing
Rua José Delalíbera, 962
86.183-550 – Cambé – PR
Email: soporte@booklas.com
www.booklas.com

Summary

Foreword 5
Chapter 1 The Art Of Divination 7
Chapter 2 Mysteries of Space/Time 14
Chapter 3 Universal Energies 21
Chapter 4 Divinatory Tools 29
Chapter 5 Cosmic Astrology 38
Chapter 6 The Gift Of Clairvoyance 47
Chapter 7 Deciphering Prophetic Dreams 56
Chapter 8 The Flow Of The Universe 62
Chapter 9 The Enigma Of Fate 70
Chapter 10 Prophecies 78
Chapter 11 The Dance of Chaos 86
Chapter 12 Timelines 92
Chapter 13 Flow Of Time 98
Chapter 14 The Depth of Infinity 104
Chapter 15 Portal to Universal Knowledge 110
Chapter 16 Revelations Of The Future 116
Chapter 17 Predictions for Humanity 122
Chapter 18 Love, Transformative Force 128
Chapter 19 Cosmic Balance 132
Chapter 20 The Fate Of The Earth 136
Chapter 21 The Depth of the Present 140
Chapter 22 Universal Unity 144
Chapter 23 The Dance of Change 148
Chapter 24 The Journey Continues 152

Epilogue Uniting Heaven And Earth 156

Foreword

In the shadows of the vast universe, where the stars dance a cosmic choreography and the secrets of time are whispered by the intergalactic wind, a transcendental path known as the Arcturian Oracle is revealed.

This book is a passage through the constellations, guiding those who seek more than visible reality, shedding light on the unknown dimensions and mysteries that await in the folds of time.

The Arcturians (beings of light and cosmic wisdom) lift the veil between the tangible and the intangible, offering glimpses of the future and profound visions of the present. This is not just a book; it is a portal to understanding the fabrics of the universe and interpreting the lines of destiny.

Enter with an open mind and a heart devoid of fear, for this book unveils the journey that transcends space and time, weaving a narrative where magic intertwines with reality. Explore the spiritual practices of the Arcturians, tune in to cosmic energies and uncover the secrets of the Oracle that transcends human limitations.

Each chapter is a doorway to a new dimension, a listening room where the whispers of the stars become inner resonances. From the awakening of consciousness to the dance of the stars, this book is an invitation to a journey beyond the confines of the known, where mystery is the guide and intuition is the compass.

Embark now, intrepid seeker, and allow the Arcturian Oracle to be your guide on the paths of the unknown. For in the pages that unfold before you, magic awaits, and the answers emerge like shooting stars in the vastness of the universe.

Chapter 1
The Art Of Divination

In the vast cosmos, orbiting the resplendent star Arcturus, lies the home planet of the Arcturians. This alien race, endowed with extraordinary abilities of clairvoyance and manipulation of space-time, traces its lineage back to the primordial dawns of the universe. The Arcturians, as they are known, have transcended the conventional boundaries of cosmic knowledge, becoming a guiding light for those who seek to understand the intricate paths of time and existence.

The Arcturians' journey begins with the supreme cosmic architects sowing the quantum seeds destined to blossom on countless worlds. Among these primordial sparks, the favorite children of Arcturus and the great destinies that awaited them were already glimpsed. The planet Arcturus Prime, a cradle of beauty and abundance, reflects the harmony and prosperity cultivated by generations of Arcturians, whose values transcend the limits of intellect, guided by intellectual discipline combined with intuitive wisdom.

The legend surrounding the mystical aura of the Arcturian people goes back to the unfathomable ages, where the promise of natural wonders blossomed on multiple worlds. In this grandiose setting, the Arcturians stand out not only for their technology, but for the unique synthesis between their technological achievements and the noble principles that permeate their society. On Arcturus Prime, calculating pragmatism intertwines with universal ethics and compassion, creating a web of values that transcends existence itself.

Generations of dedicated Arcturian scholars have perfected sophisticated systems that transcend simple cosmic observation, capturing and correlating subtle patterns between the variables that influence the probabilistic fabric of space-time. These analyses are not just distant observations, but windows into the future and the past, providing relevant insights into key trends and events with a precision that defies conventional understanding.

The technical genius of the Arcturians lies not only in advanced equipment, but in the extraordinary mental capacity of its inhabitants. From an early age, talented individuals are identified to undergo intense neuropsychic training. This journey aims not only to hone the skills of clairvoyance, precognition, hindsight and astral projection, but also to transcend into a hyper-sensory sphere. These individuals, known as "Oraculists," become masters of the art of separating their immaterial essences from their bodily wrappings, projecting their consciousnesses to any relevant times or places to gain reliable prophetic insights.

As they mature, Oraculists perform true feats of space-time ubiquity, inhabiting other bioenergetically compatible bodies. Whether in remote chronologies or artificial avatars in hyper-realistic virtual realities, these Arcturian emissaries witness probabilistic events before formalizing predictions. When they return to their original forms, they bring with them a wealth of experiences and information, catalogued and cross-referenced with computer modeling of parallel worlds to derive reliable final predictions.

Ethical instruction is intrinsic to Arcturian society. From an early age, all citizens are educated in the noble ideals that should govern the responsible use of privileged knowledge about the future. The revelation of visions is permitted only if it does not interfere prejudicially with the natural flow of events or violate elementary universal rights. This ethical commitment is reinforced by the sacred oath that each Oraculist takes to the High Psychotronic Council of the Arcturus before carrying out operations to directly capture profound temporal insights.

This ethical approach is maintained through meticulous audits by the High Council. Only approved forecasts, after rigorous ethical filters, are made available at different levels of detail. Precaution is crucial to avoid catastrophic impacts on the time stream if excessively sensitive information is revealed prematurely to unprepared civilizations.

The refined technique of the Arcturians' temporal simulation and projection equipment, although vital, represents only one facet of the oracular system. The essence lies in the Oraculists' extraordinary mental faculties.

The ability to "inhabit" other bodies and project their consciousnesses to different eras is not just a demonstration of power, but an ethical responsibility. When they return to their original forms, Oraculists bring with them not only information, but the burden of choices and experiences they have lived through on their astral missions. These experiences are systematically catalogued and cross-referenced with computer modeling of parallel worlds, resulting in predictions that transcend simple temporal linearity.

Ethics, a fundamental pillar of Arcturian society, is reinforced by the sacred oath to the High Psychotronic Council. Transparency is maintained, and each oracular operation is subjected to a careful audit by the Council's ascended masters. This process ensures that only ethical predictions, aligned with the fundamental principles, are released for consultation. The integrity of the Arcturians' oracular system is a safeguard against the misuse of privileged knowledge about the future.

However, even sincere requesters can be denied insights into specific events. The High Council, zealous for the preservation of cosmic balance, postpones or refuses revelations that could pose unacceptable risks or unjustified disturbances. Responsibility transcends individual desire; it is a safeguard against the potential abuse of oracular information for selfish interests.

Over millennia, the ethical consistency of the Arcturians in handling the boundary issues of transcendental ethics has built the unshakeable reputation of the legendary Oracle of Arcturus. Routinely requested by high-ranking members of the Grand Cosmic Council prior to the formalization of pan-dimensional resolutions, the Oracle is a reliable source of profound temporal insights. However, the careful dissemination of these predictions is crucial to avoid catastrophic disruptions in the temporal flow.

The Arcturians' predictions, although accurate, are not seen as inflexible certainties. The omniscience often attributed to them is demythologized. Even the most reliable predictions are seen as logical extrapolations derived from insights gleaned from the subtle planes of reality. Master Oraculists warn of the probabilistic nature of any manifest determinism, pointing out that some degree of uncertainty always permeates the margins of any prediction, no matter how well-founded it may seem.

To ensure a responsible approach, forecasts are shared in the most generic formats possible. The language is often ambiguous, full of metaphors and metonymies. This choice is not a limitation, but a safeguard to avoid misleading interpretations, accidental hermeneutic distortions or self-fulfilling prophecies. The predictions are offered in a carefully calibrated way to respect the free will of the recipients and minimize the risks associated with a fatalistic sense of determinism.

When consulted on matters of historical or cosmic importance, the Arcturian Oracle takes a cautious approach. On the other hand, personal matters of lesser importance receive direct or quantitative assessments, according to established protocols.

The Arcturians' predictions are often considered manifestations of omniscience, but they mainly reflect the Arcturians' ability to integrate sublime perspectives gleaned through temporal espionage techniques. Their hyper-complex simulations are based on the best science available on Arcturus Prime. Even the most reliable predictions are one of countless possible logical extrapolations, considering the unpredictable interference of choices made by sentient minds endowed with free will.

The accuracy of the Arcturians' models does not deny the probabilistic nature of manifest determinism. There is always a margin for deviations and redefinitions introduced by as yet uncharted variables and dynamic interactions. Uncertainty, however minimal, is inherent in prediction, reaffirming the unfathomable complexity of existence.

Even in the face of the extraordinary achievements of the Arcturians, scholars warn of the inevitability of dysfunctional individuals or subcultures emerging in utopian societies. For this reason, strict ethical compliance protocols permeate all sensitive activities in Arcturus. Suspected deviations are investigated with transparency and exemplary rigor by the relevant accountability agencies.

Arcturians remain dedicated to the ideal of harmony and prosperity, understanding that the journey towards evolution is dotted with obstacles. True greatness, they argue, is achieved by overcoming these challenges. The legacy of the Arcturians transcends not only their oracular abilities and technological advances, but also their continuous quest for moral excellence, solidifying their place as ethical guardians and respected mentors in the cosmic vastness.

Thus, throughout the ages, the Arcturians have earned legitimate respect and moral authority. Their impeccable example, noble values and remarkable achievements have raised the general cosmic consciousness. The oracular records, far from being an end in themselves, are a secondary by-product of unpretentious efforts to raise cosmic consciousness and offer guidance when requested.

In closing this chapter, we are left with the image of the Arcturians as an advanced society that not only predicts the future, but shapes it on the basis of ethical principles and a relentless pursuit of true greatness.

Chapter 2
Mysteries of Space/Time

As we saw in the previous chapter, the so-called "Arcturian Oracle" has its origins in a highly sophisticated technology capable of making surprisingly accurate predictions about future events, both on a personal and collective level. This extraordinary ability to "read" multiple probabilistic timelines is due to several factors, starting with the immense computing power and accurate modeling of potential realities by the Arcturian machines.

However, contrary to what some still insist on speculating, such technological equipment, however advanced, represents only one part of a deeper equation involving dimensional and quantum understandings of how time and space work.

For the Arcturians, these domains are not isolated variables or merely physical phenomena perceptible to the primary human senses. They are both part of a single multidimensional energy matrix that encompasses matter, mind and spirit in an integrated way, as sides of the same cosmic coin.

On this underlying plane that governs the concrete manifestation of events as we perceive them, time and space dissolve their usually rigid boundaries to acquire much more fluid, holographic and interchangeable contours through incursions into parallel realities and alternative lines of temporal probability.

Thus, what we call the "future" is nothing more than an illusory linear projection created by the human mind, which is still bound by the limits of perceiving the "now" as always sliding from the "before" towards the "after".

However, freed from the three-dimensional restraints imposed by the physical brain, the expanded spirit of the Arcturians is able to experience remote futures and distant pasts no longer as separate segments along a fixed timeline, but as interconnected fields of consciousness available for immediate access through quantum dives.

By entering this heightened state of transcendental perception, trained Arcturian prophets can literally tune in, feel, confabulate and even interact with their own projected versions as alternative consciousnesses, experiencing multiple probabilistic paths forward in time.

Such points of future experience are not randomly dispersed, but often self-organized into complex multidimensional networks of quantumly overlapping nodes or realities that would look very much like gigantic fractals eventually manifested on the physical plane by derivation from their own self-similar holographic nature.

By deeply understanding such key principles about the fundamental unreality of chronological time and the underlying simultaneity of all infinite possibilities coexisting in a potential state, psychics are able to "read" future events on the subtle planes with the same level of clarity and proximity as they access memories of their own past in our ordinary minds.

Equipped with such transcendent eidetic faculties, prophets can even identify and characterize with recognizable taxonomies and terminologies the main archetypes, personas or "characters" of these plots eventually destined to densify in our consensual reality from their previously visualized quantum sketches.

This is where the Arcturian computer simulations come in, which meticulously analyze all the variables involved to calculate the relative probabilities of these "future potentials" seen by the seers actually becoming consolidated as the real future to be manifested.

In order to filter out the "signal" of these visions from the imaginary subjective "noise" that might contaminate them, countless cross-checks are made between the predictions of various trained prophets before any major prognosis is formalized and recorded by the Arcturian Oracle.

Reaching very high degrees of consensus between various visionaries and complex computer models, these filtered prognoses are given the seal of authenticity by the High Psychotronic Council of the Arcturians before being categorized by their degree of reliability and shared externally when appropriate.

Among the countless referenced predictions kept in the Arcturian historical records, they range from personal consultations with nobles from amalgamated civilizations to advice on significant events for entire worlds, such as mass migrations from adverse climates or the rise and fall of empires over the centuries.

Even on Earth, there are recurring cases of influential groups who have secretly made crucial decisions based on oracular consultation with the Arcturians, be they great political and religious leaders or even obscure initiatic societies with privileged knowledge about the future of humanity.

Certainly the fact that the Arcturian astral archives hold such remote and precise information about so many peoples, planets and civilizations arouses the curiosity of those who dedicate themselves to studying their impressive predictive techniques. Could it be that these records were produced with such millimetre accuracy by means of extreme magnification of the already fantastic clairvoyant ability of their seers to observe the distant past when they consult the deep future during their hyperdimensional dives? Or perhaps, as a considerable number of Oracle scholars speculate, there are even more exotic phenomena behind this apparent transgenerational omniscience manifested by the accurate records of eras whose direct and indirect witnesses have long since returned to the cosmic dust?

According to these researchers, it would be possible that in their psychospatial explorations, talented Arcturian projectionists could not only access any temporal coordinates as immaterial observers, as long as they appropriately calibrate the "frequency" of their extracorporeal consciousnesses to compatible vibrational parameters. But it is speculated that some very advanced seers could go even further, using this same principle of "dimensional tuning" no longer to visit specific sections of holo-history, but to actually physically incarnate in any timeline of interest before then returning to their native eras of origin.

If confirmed, such a hypothesis would set truly revolutionary precedents, even for the already astonishing standards of trans-dimensional manipulation exhibited by these angelic beings, descendants of the first sparks beyond the Dimensional Void, which would one day form all matter and life currently organized in countless parallel universes. For such abilities would imply that, through successive "quantum infiltrations" carried out by expert seers in the remote past of specific worlds, all the necessary direct experience could be acquired through multiple incarnations located in the chronologies of interest to then bring such lived records back to the native eras of these temporal agents in the future of their own original causal line.

Equipped with such personal and unquestionable experiential records, Arcturian mnemonic-historians would be able to compose impeccably accurate past analyses even of epochs whose direct participants and all their works have long since faded into the sunset of time, as a local continuum eventually destined to experience quantum redefinitions of identity or simply be reborn in superior parallel realities less limited in their spatio-temporal coherences.

It seems, therefore, that such are the extraordinary gifts of Arcturian seers: freed from the grids of rigid chronological linearity in their astral journeys, able to float through any past or future coordinates, foreseeing distant events, or physically incarnating to experience remote eras in person before returning their essences home in the future. The prophetic children of Arcturus even seem to be curators of historical records of unprecedented accuracy, integrating multiple realities and guaranteeing absolute fidelity in their chronicles thanks to these unique talents of temporal and multidimensional ubiquity.

In possession of such vast and precise collections, the next analytical efforts simply involve compiling, correlating and extrapolating trends from this monumental base of temporal Big Data available in their oracular banks to produce comprehensive socio-cultural forecasts. For this reason, the proverbial casual assertiveness of the Arcturian Oracle remains unbeatable, even when tested against independent oracular control groups spread across the Federation, and is informally adopted as a kind of prophetic "gold standard", on which even other respected tutelary entities, such as the haughty Orientals of Aldebaran or the Ascended sages of Pleyades, request consultations before formulating their own externally disseminated cosmic predictions.

There is even a particular belief among some primitive peoples on the outskirts of the Galaxy that the legendary Oracle of the Arcturians is actually a centuries-old system bequeathed by ancestral progenitors of the current Arcturian civilization, so old that it dates back to the very beginnings of the local universe, when the first shoots of sentient life were still crawling in their notions of causality and determinism, among materialized simulacra newly conceived to house their minds in formation, newly awakened from the primeval thinking forms of the Universal Being, filtered from the Higher Planes of the Primordial Cosmic Consciousness and their individual sparks of fragmentation.

Even if such adverse speculations seem unlikely, given the proven mastery of today's Arcturians, they at least illustrate how extraordinary and even bizarre by ordinary cosmic standards are the oracular faculties displayed by these veteran angelic beings.

In fact, everything leads one to believe that the unparalleled quality of such prophetic projections is due primarily to the excellence of the sensory, intellectual, pandimensional and technical processes combined in their total operation, allowing them to capture, correlate and extrapolate the whole range of nuances determining the definition of each line of manifestable potential with a degree of resolution and accuracy not yet satisfactorily replicated even by powerful artificial Intelligences from advanced worlds dedicated to Probabilistic Forecasting in Deep Time.

Chapter 3
Universal Energies

As explained in previous chapters, the "Arcturian Oracle" is much more than an elaborate technological system of probabilistic prediction. In fact, its functioning depends primarily on the harmonious connection with what the seers describe simply as "the Universal Energies".

But what exactly are these "Universal Energies" that are so decisive in enabling oracular readings of such impressive accuracy, even by hyper-advanced galactic standards?

Immediately, the Arcturians' own explanations already advance some crucial points: such Energies would not constitute an abstract or random mystical force. On the contrary, they manifest themselves through extra-physical patterns and cycles of an essentially fractal, holographic and, above all, conscious nature. Thus, in order to better understand his narrative, we need to temporarily expand our horizons beyond the classical Newtonian vision that still delimits modern scientific thought on Earth, because the fundamental principles that govern multidimensional reality in the Arcturian perspective simply transcend conventional notions of linear causality.

According to their cosmogenesis, our observable universe would be nothing more than a previously imperceptible material by-product of energetic, informational and consciential flows generated from subtler planes, but causally ontologically prior to ordinary space-time manifestation itself. From a non-religious perspective, we could poetically compare such planes to a kind of Primordial Cosmic Protoconsciousness, a pre-material Fundamental Intelligence that would have gradually differentiated into myriad individual subconsciousnesses as it emanated its creative influx through the densest strata of manifest reality. In this perpetual process of exteriorization, each individualized consciential spark would end up shaping its own internal universe and, by twilight projection, materializing different space-time textures, where they would then start to interact with each other under varying degrees of self-consciousness and even incarnation in specific sub-universes like ours.

Naturally, given this unified ancestral common origin, these apparently individualized streams of consciousness would inevitably remain interconnected through their very subtle non-local roots, which permeate across all strata and manifest realities down to the densest physical plane shaped by their descendant conscious creations. This is the essence of the Arcturian conception of the so-called "Universal Energies": they are multidimensional inflows radiating from these primarily hyperdimensional superconscious planes towards the lower strata of perceptible manifestation. Flowing through everything that constitutes the physical worlds and their inhabitants, these archetypal energies would not represent blind forces, but highly intelligent currents of information, consciousness and even creative intent - conscious morphogenetic codes capable of condensing forms, events and even entire civilizations when attracted and organized by the gravitational fields generated around complex foci of manifest consciousness, such as planetary or galactic incarnations.

In this context, the very self-similar fractal structure observable in most natural phenomena would result from this perpetually renewed directional flow of interconnected individual consciousnesses projecting their common essence onto different substrates through analogous cyclical processes of creative interiorization and exteriorization. In other words, the Arcturians explain the characteristic codes repetitively embedded in nature as the reflection of pre-existing universal archetypal patterns in the primordial collective superconscious which then express themselves imagistically through the various created realities - all of which holographically contain in their own most elementary atomic structures the "genes" of the diverse whole from which their relative temporal existence emanates. Following this emanationist logic, the astrological cycles so meticulously mapped out by ancient terrestrial esoteric schools would also be nothing more than external epiphanies of these multidimensional internal influxes occurring at sub-quantum levels between planes directly responsible for the very continuous genesis of ever-renewed micro- and macro-microsms. In short, in the Arcturian vision, all dimensions of perceivable existence would literally be immersed in this vast ocean of archetypal universal energies indelibly imprinted on them through all kinds of nested cycles, invariably bringing the patterns of the underlying One Essence to the surface through the myriad relative forms it takes on. And it would be precisely through these hyperdimensional channels, irrigating across the space-time consensus fabric, that trained Arcturian sensitives would be able to catch glimpses of the ever-present future-in-power destined to reveal itself in the outer now, through the continuous unfolding of these pattern-oriented formative forces of unbreakable natural order, in their eternally reinvented flow.

Like conscious fish swimming in the universal current, clairvoyants would simply learn from an early age to detect the characteristic energetic signatures preceding imminent manifestations of future realities already in an advanced stage of gestation within their still pre-material proto-dimensional cocoons. Psychometric readings of the relative qualities and volumes of these multidimensional information flows would to some extent 'announce' complex events and forms about to materialize densely through successive derivations from these highly illuminated superconscious sources, eternally unfolding their shaping influxes. In order to translate these perceptions into comprehensible terms, we then resort to precise multidimensional computer modeling capable of integrating countless quantum variables and trends detected by the hyper-developed sensory faculties of these Arcturian Ascended Masters.

Thanks to this exceptional conjunction of clairvoyant gifts, oracular technology and deep theoretical understanding of the space-time continuum as a dynamic hologram projected from previous consciential planes, the so-called Arcturian Oracle has built its well-deserved reputation as a singularly accurate prophetic device even by the hyper-advanced standards prevailing in this region of the local universe.

However, as the Hermetic wisdom teaches, "as below so above", the same universally valid fractal principles allow seers to foresee macro manifesting patterns that cyclically also operate in microcosmic spheres of reality.

Indeed, although its predominant focus lies on collectively consensual events of broad civilizational interest, the Oracle has traditionally been used on a smaller scale to make predictions and issue personalized advice on an individual level to those willing to follow the suggested preventive guidelines with courage and determination.

There are countless historical examples, from humble commoners who received a few months' notice of impending natural disasters or conflicts in their regions, and were then able to prepare and temporarily emigrate to safe areas, to powerful sovereigns and planetary rulers who would have avoided assassinations, palace intrigues or military defeats by taking various preventative decisions after consulting the fearsome Oracle of the Arcturians through ambassadors and astral messengers.

However, just as in most collective cases, the chances of individual success also increase significantly depending on the degree of internal understanding, moral virtue and determination to align thoughts, feelings and actions according to the realignments suggested by oracular consultations precisely customized to the needs of each particular case.

After all, even for such advanced technology, it is mathematically impossible to generate absolutely assertive personalized predictions without first establishing deep and stable energetic connections with each individual consulting consciousness in order to define minimum synchronistic parameters capable of anchoring within acceptable margins the complex spectrum of variables imaginable for each unique biological host and their myriad imaginable probabilistic crossroads expanding their potential personal realities into fractals.

However, once such a deep connection has been firmly established through successive consultations and the consulter's proven emotional and intellectual receptiveness to the preliminary studies revealed, Arcturian analysts progressively become capable of generating highly personalized insights and suggestions with an increasing chance of assertiveness even on delicate matters involving health, relationships, career and other issues crucial to individual destinies.

Extraordinary examples include countless recorded cases of terminally ill patients who have recovered after following the Oracle's personalized treatment recommendations, couples in borderline situations whose relationships have been reinvigorated after reconsidering important decisions made in haste, or even social outcasts who have completely reversed their life stories by receiving precious guidance on choices and priorities never before considered in their usually defeatist moods and outlooks.

Although it may sound unreasonable for a civilization that is still largely materialistic like the contemporary terrestrial one, everything indicates that the healing or deterioration of any manifest biological system results primarily from the energetic and informational influxes projected from its inner consciential host through its densified outer envelopes.

Following this line of reasoning, which is coherent with the holographic principles previously elucidated, reformulating such deep personal patterns of self-belief and self-materializing expectations through synchronistic interventions such as the predictions and advice issued by the Arcturian Oracle would have the ability to subatomically redefine the very subtle and dense energy matrix responsible for shaping, within the established inner limits, the viable spectrum of probable physical experiences to unfold on each individual's unique path in the shared common consensual time.

In short, whether at the individual microcosmic level or the collective macrocosm, the modus operandi behind the astonishing rates of oracular precision that have been repeatedly confirmed seems to stem from this unique ability to apprehend informational influxes and tendencies at a germinal stage not yet manifested just below the threshold of ordinary perception and then translate them analytically into terms palatable to the patterns of mechanistic causality still dominant at the current stage of consulting civilizations.

As multidimensional unfoldings of the same One Essence on its primordial archetypal planes, the connection internally recognized as an individualized identity with this consciential continuum common to everything and all beings, seems to give Arcturian Initiates the privilege of foreseeing future probabilities, both internal and external, with an impressive degree of penetration and assertiveness that is still little understood.

Chapter 4
Divinatory Tools

Among the most sacred instruments used by Arcturian seers to perform their divinations through the Oracle are those known as Vhyr-Taerya, or Divinatory Tools. They are true energetic extensions of their expanded minds capable of picking up hidden patterns in the fabric of space-time.

The Vhyr-Taerya act as catalysts that enhance the Arcturians' innate psychic abilities, allowing them to access glimpses of distant events in the past and future, which are then interpreted in the light of their extensive mystical knowledge.

According to Arcturian tradition, the Vhyr-Taerya were a gift from the Kryonn, a crystalline alien race with high spiritual wisdom. Because they live on a subtle dimensional plane, the Kryonn rarely interact directly with humanoids. But they made an exception with the Arcturians to give them these instruments.

It is said that after centuries of observing the virtuous evolution of the Arcturians and their quest to unravel the enigmas of the universe, the Kryonn took pity on them and decided to give them the Vhyr-Taerya to accelerate the awakening of their minds and better use their free will for cosmic benefit.

In fact, since they began to incorporate the use of the Vhyr-Taerya into their oracular practices, the Arcturian priests have greatly increased the scope and accuracy of their astral predictions, becoming an essential reference point among people interested in the divinatory arts.

Initially, the Kryonn bequeathed the Arcturians seven main Vhyr-Taerya, a number that carries strong esoteric symbolism in their culture. Later, the Arcturians themselves developed new hybrid tools, combining special crystals with noble metals and alchemical alloys in compound recipes, the details of which remain secret.

The original seven Vhyr-Taerya remain revered as the most sacred and are used to this day in the most important divinatory rituals performed by Arcturian seers within the Qrnil G temples, spread across the twelve planets that orbit the Arcturus Star in the Alpha Boötis star system. The first of these is the Silver Atlantean, a triangular-shaped silver pendulum that swings over three-dimensional star maps projecting lines of light that signal places of astro-historical importance, allowing seers to reconstruct events from the past in great detail.

Another original Vhyr-Taerya worth mentioning is the Thyorium Cauldron, a heptagonal-shaped chalice engraved with glyphs on its exterior that has the property of spontaneously boiling every time it is immersed in boiling water during solstices and eclipses.

The intensity of the boiling and the coloring of the water allows us to predict the intensity and types of cosmic and social events that will tend to occur before the next temporal alignment. The denser the vapor cloud and the purpler the water, the more challenging the events tend to be.

Another craft item often used in conjunction with the Thyorium Cauldron to enhance results is the Vharian Medallion, a necklace with a dark crystal pendant that works as a frequency transducer for the surrounding electromagnetic field.

When immersed in boiling water after rituals with the Cauldron, the Medallion captures and temporarily stores subtle information in its crystal, which is then accessed telepathically by psychics in a meditative state. The messages captured are presented as dreamlike images of landscapes with spatial folds that reveal symbolic panoramas of events to come. Interpreting the symbolism of the elements observed in these visions requires extensive training in the Arcturian psyche.

Another extremely valuable original tool for the Arcturians is the Orb of Chronoss, a sphere of glass-like material surrounded by two concentric rings that rotate around the luminous orb, generating a radial gravitational field capable of bending the timelines. By gazing meditatively into the hypnotic vortex created by the synchronized movement of Chronoss, Arcturian seers are able to clearly glimpse environmental panoramas from different periods of the past and future, thus obtaining remote visions of parallel worlds.

The Divinatory Drum of Arghhonatz, on the other hand, consists of a sacred musical instrument whose construction secretly involves metals and minerals only found in the caves of Galh-Styynz, a mythical mountain of crystals located inside Arcturus IV, one of the twelve planets orbiting the Arcturus Star.

As it is rhythmically percussed, the Drum emits special vibrating frequencies capable of amplifying brain waves, opening dormant psychic channels in the minds of the seers and allowing them to access past lives related both to their own existence in the universal quantum field and that of other consulting beings.

Among all the original instruments bequeathed by Kryonn, however, the most impressive Vhyr-Taerya according to the Arcturians is the Interdimensional Telescope, a kind of prismatic telescope made of lapis lazuli and special crystals that allows one to see into black holes, distant galaxies and even parallel worlds outside the known electromagnetic spectrum.

Looking through the telescope during certain planetary alignments generates in the expanded minds of Arcturian seers visions of multidimensional kaleidoscopes with myriad galaxies and humanoid constellations coexisting at different civilizational stages beyond the terrestrial human plane, thus allowing them to foresee potential destinies awaiting the human race on its evolutionary journey.

In addition to these seven original Vhyr-Taerya, over time the Arcturians themselves have developed dozens of other extremely elaborate hybrid divinatory tools, which incorporate various gems, minerals and special metals in their making.

The alchemical sophistication involved in such instruments is considered secret, even by Arcturian standards, and their use is reserved only for the most senior hierophants of the astrological order in the rituals of time held within the Temple of G'rhynzul on the planet Arcturus Prime.

Among these post-Kryonian hybrid tools, the one that most impresses consultants from other worlds is the Animatus Star Map, a three-dimensional representation of the Milky Way made of liquid crystal and magnetite powder with supernatural properties. The Map has the astonishing ability to display hyper-realistic animations of the movement of the entire galaxy from an external perspective on its surface, accelerating from the present to the future at varying speeds according to the settings manipulated by the psychics during the consultations. By pausing the animation at a given point in the future, the map reveals the position and appearance of all the stars at that point in space-time, allowing the Arcturians to make analyses and predictions based on the probable energetic effects of the stellar alignments on the adjacent cosmic quadrants.

Another piece of impressive beauty and oracular power is the Planetarium of Vhyprianus, a miniature replica of the planetary system of Arcturus with each world represented by a precious gemstone engraved with mystical symbols and related magical properties. The twelve miniature worlds orbit the large central diamond sphere representing Arcturus, the whole composition spinning gently supported by the antigravity field of a palladium cube.

When approaching the Planetarium during consultations, Arcturian seers can detect subtle variations in the trajectories of the gems, as well as temporary fulgurations and eclipses that transmit ciphered information to them about imminent or ongoing events in the different worlds, allowing for preventative or corrective action.

There is also the Projector Orb, a hollow sphere of koruum (liquid silver) graduated with alchemical markings and numerological runes whose interior contains a reversed crystalline zero-field fluid. When shaken and thrown by seers during special augurs, the Orb floats in the air projecting rays of light that form three-dimensional images of beings and events belonging to various alternative timelines.

Interpreting this miscellany of random scenes requires contextualizing it within Arcturian symbolism, but it can reveal connections between apparently unconnected variables, making it possible to foresee high-impact events even on planes far from the seers' present visual field.

Another mystical object of great relevance during the oracular work of the Arcturian high hierophants is the Drum of Vhyprius, made of a fused metal alloy of silver, cobalt, iron and carbon, with unique sound properties.

Its shape resembles a starry dodecahedron, with pentagonal faces engraved with luminescent glyphs. When struck rhythmically, it emits isochronic frequencies that induce changes in consciousness, allowing precise channeling of entities and messages from parallel planes materialized in the form of quantum scriptures.

These messages bring valuable guidance and ancestral advice for dilemmas faced by both the Arcturian civilization and other cultures with whom they establish contact in a mutual exchange of learning throughout the stellar ages.

Worthy of note is the Atlantean Medallion, a diamond-shaped piece made of kelzon, a crystal capable of storing and amplifying astral energies. It contains sealed water from the oceans of Lhyrenzius, a legendary oceanic planet that is said to have existed where the Asteroid Belt is today.

According to ancient stellar records, Lhyrenzius was destroyed by successive collisions of meteors attracted by its intense electromagnetic field. However, before its complete disintegration, Lhyrenzian sages were said to have collected vital essences now preserved in the Medallion as reliquary quantum information from worlds to be reawakened.

By immersing the Medallion in energetic sources during consultations at the G'rhynzul Temple, Hierophants are able to access Lhyrenzian wisdom in the form of telepathic insights with instructive revelations about the holo-world challenges that permeate the transitions between cosmic eras in the evolutionary processes of sentient planets.

Another magnificent piece is the Celestióculo de Italh-Bren, an intricate celestial globe made of transparent amoroso crystals mounted on a frame of kripturium, an antigravitational metal, with the ability to float above energized pools projecting three-dimensional star holograms indicating probable changes in the course of stars and possible collisions.

By manipulating the Celestióculo's internal structures through mentally transmitted codes, Hierophants can accelerate the holographic projection and thus visualize the relative position of stars and planets at any future point in space-time, even beyond the event horizon predictable by traditional Arcturian astrology techniques.

This makes it possible not only to foresee and guard against potential meteorological or seismic catastrophes of greater magnitude, but also to choose the most suitable times to host The Great Conclaves of the Enlightened Minds of Arcturus, events in which the hierophants of Alpha Boötis receive representatives from other stellar cultures for mutual exchanges of multi-dimensional knowledge aimed at the spiritual progress of the entire galactic community.

The most exotic of all Arcturian divinatory tools, however, is what has become known as the Khaa'Lynrian Chrono-Comprehender, a kind of semi-organic machine telepathically connected to the consciousness of the Temple of G'rhynzul.

Through intricate systems of piezoelectric crystals and superconducting metals, the Chrono-Comprehender is able to detect subtle chronotronic anomalies caused whenever dimensional travelers from the future interact with the present anywhere in the multiverse, issuing alerts that allow the Hierophants to identify and interpret even minimal potential impacts caused by such anonymous visitors, determining preventive measures whenever necessary.

According to speculation never officially confirmed by the Hierophant Guardians of the Mysteriorum Arcturianum themselves, the Khaa'Lynrian Chrono-Understander would actually be a gift from the semi-legendary people known only as The Fixers of Ages.

Legend has it that The Eras Fixers constitute a trans-dimensional order responsible for ensuring the consolidation and preservation of the predominant timelines that will form the official akashic record at the end of each local planetary era.

To do this, they constantly monitor clashes between renegade chronologists bent on rewriting events from the past in order to cause temporal bifurcations that will have a significant impact on the future development of civilizations. Awarding the Chrono-Comprehender to the Arcturians would therefore be a gesture of recognition for their noble mission to maintain the temporal balance and protect the natural flow of cosmic evolution.

When exploring the Vhyr-Taerya, from the original seven to the elaborate hybrid divinatory tools, it becomes clear that the Arcturians developed a deep symbiosis with these instruments. Mastery of these tools not only enriched their oracular practices, but also strengthened the connection between Arcturian seers and the cosmic forces that govern the universe.

Chapter 5
Cosmic Astrology

Cosmic astrology is one of the most profound and sacred forms of divination used by the Arcturians in their legendary Oracle. It interprets the movements and alignments of the celestial bodies to reveal the designs of the universe and unravel the mysteries of the future.

The Arcturians believe that the stars exert a powerful energetic influence on all beings. Each planet and star emits unique electromagnetic frequencies that interact with the auric fields of living beings, altering their realities.

By carefully observing the cosmic choreography of the stars, the Arcturians decipher a subtle and symbolic language that holds keys to understanding the temporal cycles that govern existence. It's as if the starry sky were narrating, in silent poetry, the events to come.

For the Arcturians, the Earth and the entire solar system are intrinsically interconnected in a multidimensional energy web. What affects one has repercussions for all; no cosmic phenomenon occurs in isolation.

In this way, by interpreting a particular alignment or planetary movement, the Arcturians can extract comprehensive predictions, ranging from climatic and social events on Earth to dimensional transformations on a cosmic level.

One of the foundations of cosmic astrology lies in the careful observation of the cycles between the celestial bodies. The Arcturians follow the revolutions, orbits, synchronicities and encounters between planets, moons, suns and stars with ancient knowledge. These cycles reveal hidden patterns about the cosmic ages through which the universe passes in its eternal existence. Like the earth's zodiac wheel, there are larger wheels governing kalpas, i.e. cycles of millions or billions of years.

The Arcturians say, for example, that the Earth's current alignment with the center of the galaxy will profoundly affect humanity, bringing intense spiritual acceleration and widening of consciousness in the coming centuries. It is the awakening to a new cosmic era. Another important star used by the Arcturians in their cosmic astrology is Alcyone; the Central Sun. It is the main star of the Pleiades constellation, considered the home of the seven sidereal sisters in Greek mythology.

According to Arcturian teachings, when Alcyone emits intense emanations of light and aligns magnetically with our Sun, interdimensional portals are opened through which highly evolved beings transit on a mission to Earth.

Jesus is said to have received a direct influx of light from Alcyone at his birth, which extraordinarily amplified his spiritual powers and made him an avatar of the new cosmic era on Earth. Other masters and prophets are also said to have received blessings from Alcyone.

When it comes to the constellations and their mythologies, the Arcturians find rich symbolisms and prophecies about human trajectory. For example, the constellation of Scorpio and its legend are interpreted as a reference to the adversities that humanity would face on its evolutionary journey.

But for the Arcturians, the constellation of Aquarius and its golden age symbolism represent the times to come. The current process of transition of the Earth's zodiac to this age, with the passing of the ages from Pisces to Aquarius, would indicate profound socio-cultural transformations on Earth.

Certain astronomical events and phenomena much awaited by Arcturian astrologers are lunar and solar eclipses. For them, such events demarcate intersections between planes and dimensions, allowing the subtle perception of parallel realities during the temporary lines in which the Moon covers the Sun or the Earth casts its shadow on the Moon.

During a lunar eclipse, for example, a multidimensional cosmic cone is formed whose apex coincides with the exact location of the Moon at the time of the phenomenon. This unique interdimensional portal allows Arcturians to project their consciousness into parallel realities, foreseeing certain future events.

In solar eclipses, the Arcturians interpret the symbolism of the projected shadow as a representation of the adversities that periodically obscure the sun's light, bringing stagnation and decay before the evolutionary leaps, but after each solar eclipse, the light of progress returns intensified.

Another important cosmic marker in Arcturian astrology are the equinoxes and solstices, i.e. the times of year when day and night are of equal length on Earth and when the longest days and shortest nights of the year occur, respectively.

According to the Arcturians, the equinoxes and solstices mark energetic intersections between spiritual dimensions that influence earthly events. For this reason, these dates are ideal for contacting higher planes and obtaining glimpses of extraphysical realities and future events.

The legendary predictions contained in the Arcturian Oracle are obtained by carefully observing all these celestial events and markers, as well as their cycles, translations and synchronicities.

Armed with ancestral knowledge of the symbolism of each star and cosmic phenomenon, the Arcturian seers weave intricate interpretations that synthesize, in comprehensive vaticinations, the movement of the great cosmic wheel that governs the destinies of the universe.

However, despite the deterministic tone, the Arcturians emphasize that astrological predictions contain elements of unpredictability, given the free will of beings as a variable that cannot be completely mapped in any divination where the universe would resemble a complex multidimensional network of infinite possibilities. At each point of intersection of this network there are future bifurcations, in which all potentialities are contained in a state of quantum superposition.

In this way, until a given potentiality materializes on a given dimensional plane, as a result of acts of conscious will, all possibilities still remain as embryonic futures in parallel.

Arcturian seers point out that the act of predicting a certain timeline does not invalidate or eliminate the concomitant existence of the others. What is done is to start from fractal patterns perceived in the movements of the cosmos to indicate the sequences most likely to manifest. This is why, throughout their stellar history, some of the Arcturians' astrological prophecies have not come true exactly as predicted. Not because their predictive abilities were limited, but because they used their free will to forge new realities.

However, given the multidimensional wisdom of the Arcturians, even these apparent inaccuracies end up finding interpretations and re-readings in hermeneutic spirals of meaning, in an eternal search for the definitive explanation within the Oracle.

One example of an unfulfilled prophecy gaining new interpretations is the famous prediction that the planet Nibiru or Planet X would collide with Earth at the end of the 20th century, causing a severe planetary cataclysm. Obviously, such a collision never occurred, which led to disbelief and skepticism about the

Arcturians' astrological abilities. However, they reaffirm that there was indeed such potential, but that humanity's collective consciousness was raised enough to manifest an alternative timeline.

The Arcturians argue that the prophecy itself generated positive energetic movements, leading millions of souls to prayers, meditations and loving emanations that would have subtly TRANSFORMED Nibiru's trajectory away from Earth. As Arcturian astrology deals with interdimensional astronomy and extraphysical frequencies, it is difficult to fully prove or disprove such readings. Regardless, however, they are alternative visions that stimulate the expansion of consciousness and critical thinking.

Some of the most respected Arcturian seers of the past were Izno, Akensio, Thyoria and Vhozanus. Each of them produced monumental works bringing together astrological analyses and prophecies that reverberate to this day as references in the Arcturian mystical universe.

Izno, for example, lived during the height of Atlantean civilization on Earth. He made geographical and sociological descriptions of the lost continent that proved to be astonishingly accurate with the passage of time and the discovery of archaeological remains thousands of years later.

Akensio, on the other hand, is regarded as one of the philosophical mentors of the sovereigns who ruled Ancient Egypt for 30 dynasties. It is said that he used his visions of celestial markers such as the flooding of the Nile to advise the Pharaohs in making decisions about suitable times for planting, harvesting, sailing and building.

The seer Thyoria lived in the Mayan civilization and produced one of the most detailed mappings on the astrology of Venus, including descriptions of Kas-Vhuun, the legendary second moon of this planet, destroyed in ancient times but still visible to Arcturian eyes. Astrologer Vhozanus, on the other hand, is considered to be the most direct living portal to the consciousness of Osiris, the Egyptian deity considered to be a manifestation of the Solar Logos. It was Vhozanus who revealed the secret of the Chamber of Alignment inside the Sphinx, channeling information directly from the mind of Osiris about the interdimensional structure of the monument and its functioning. The chamber in question is a kind of portal which, when activated at times of certain astronomical alignments, amplifies cosmic energies capable of expanding consciousness and revealing secrets of the universe to initiates who meditate inside.

The extent of these revelations depends, however, on the vibrational purity and harmonic synchronization of the human mind with the cosmic frequencies captured by the Alignment Chamber inside the Sphinx. Therefore, Arcturian astrology goes far beyond simply predicting destiny. It works with the manipulation of subtle energetic forces which, properly decoded and harmoniously integrated, raise both the keen insight into the future and the levels of consciousness of those who wield them.

And this is the true objective behind the mystical Arcturian Oracle: to provide sensitizing tools capable of tuning human perception with the extraphysical dimensions that make up the plot hidden beneath the illusory veil of known holographic reality.

Only when humanity reawakens its innate telepathy with the rhythms of the cosmos will it be able to consciously participate in the act of weaving the threads of its historical journey, manifesting the scenarios it decides on through empathic harmonization and no longer through distracting dissonance.

According to the Arcturian seers, the more humans awaken this holistic consciousness and apply the knowledge contained in the Arcturian Oracle, the faster the Earth will achieve the vibrational synchronicity needed to ascend to the astrological golden age predicted so long ago in the stellar akashic records. And the main ingredient for accelerating this planetary journey towards the solar stage, the next evolutionary step for any earthly civilization, is the intentional emission of loving vibrations by the more human hearts the better, because love automatically tunes in to the high frequencies of the ascending dimensions.

Therefore, while the greater cycles of the cosmos continue their incessant flow orchestrating the stellar eras, humanity holds in its hands and hearts the power to write the destiny it decides to assume in total alignment with its most sublime spiritual potentialities.

And the first step on this journey of awakening is undoubtedly to seek to internalize the Christic, universal and timeless knowledge contained between the lines of the Arcturian Oracle, a true multidimensional portal to the mysteries of the universe in its infinite holographic manifestations across time and space.

Chapter 6
The Gift Of Clairvoyance

Among the remarkable extrasensory abilities developed by the Arcturian mind in its continuous expansions of consciousness, one of the most impressive is the mastery of clairvoyance, the ability to see events distant in time and space with an impressive level of detail.

Through clairvoyance, Arcturian seers are able to accurately glimpse scenes from the past and the future, gaining valuable insights into the causes and consequences of events still in gestation in the quantum ocean of potentialities. This is because, according to Arcturian cosmology, the past, present and future coexist simultaneously as probabilistic fields in the fabric of space-time. Therefore, by expanding their consciousness beyond the apparent barriers between these fields, the clairvoyant can catch glimpses of the underlying realities.

These visions of the future, however, are not limited to events on this earthly material plane. They range from episodes taking place in other worlds and parallel dimensions to celestial phenomena, such as the birth or collapse of distant stars and galaxies. This is because Arcturian cosmology operates with a fractal and holophonic concept of multidimensional parallel universes, mirroring and co-creating each other through synchronous axes undetectable by modern terrestrial physics. Thus, by expanding their fields of consciousness beyond the ordinary electromagnetic spectrum, Arcturian clairvoyants tune into these transdimensional axes, picking up non-local spatio-temporal insights into the past and future of both intra- and extraphysical realities. The process intensifies exponentially when these visions are obtained during oracular consultations in energized places such as the Temple of G'rhynzul or at the Arcturian Vortices scattered throughout the twelve worlds orbiting Arcturus Star.

The Arcturian Vortices are semi-crystalline rock formations that radiate amplified telepathic frequencies that enhance any latent abilities in sensitive visitors. They function as an interdimensional portal.

By approaching these vortices or focusing their mental attention on them during oracular rituals, Arcturian clairvoyants access what can be described as an "imagistic radio theater" of the past and future on multiple dimensional levels beyond the known spectrum. The impressions captured are presented as complex and dynamic scenes, which are meticulously interpreted in the light of the Arcturian clairvoyants' extensive knowledge of the symbolic languages of the local collective unconscious and the alchemical patterns of the constituent elements of the manifested universe.

One of the most respected masters of Arcturian clairvoyance was the aforementioned Seer Vhozanus, a specialist in direct psychographic channeling of entities from the extraterrestrial pantheon such as Osiris and Khmu-Ra, obtaining valuable esoteric revelations and warnings about critical events.

It is said that during one of his oracular sessions at the Great Arcturian Vortex located on the Soorthyn Satellite, Vhozanus obtained an extraordinary clairvoyant vision of the bombing and destruction of a major port city on Earth that would take place over a hundred years later. The precise description of the strange flying devices and the explosive weapons used by the attackers allowed Arcturian historians to later identify it as the Bombing of Guernica, which took place in 1937 during the Spanish Civil War.

This is just one of countless historical cases in which the impressive clairvoyant abilities of Arcturian seers made it possible to foresee and later elucidate the fateful details of tragedies or catastrophes even before the apparent causes of the events had been gestated in the present.

Another area in which Arcturian clairvoyance often excels is in preventing climatic or seismic disasters of great magnitude on inhabited worlds.

Thanks to their participation or membership in the Great Galactic Council, Arcturians regularly share clairvoyant projections of their psychographies with other advanced civilizations. In addition, they gain first-hand access to dimensional transposition, gravitational shielding and climate control technologies capable of mitigating or neutralizing the predicted effects of natural disasters.

However, the Arcturian masters warn that, however impressive such demonstrations of apparently supernatural omniscience may seem, we must not lose our humility before the designs of the mystery, because in the final analysis, all knowledge only reflects and refracts infinitesimal blocks of the wisdom emanating from the Universal Creator Source, and there always remains much more that is unknown than the little that is decoded. Furthermore, the Hierophants, Guardians of the Ancestral Teachings, point out that no clairvoyance can predict future developments with absolute certainty, due to the ever-present factor of individual and collective free will, considered to be the Catalytic Variable of the Options of Destiny. This means, as already discussed in previous sections of this oracular compendium, that all so-called "prophecies" must be seen by their recipients as mere projections of probabilities, not fait accompli.

Seers can indicate with a high degree of accuracy which outcomes are likely to manifest if certain behaviors or collective decisions prevail in a given social group at a certain moment in linear space-time. However, they emphasize that no future outcome can be considered inescapably determined, because at any moment a sudden change in the orientation of group free will can trigger new causalities capable of generating a timeline diametrically opposed to that predicted by clairvoyants.

And the closer the prediction is to the points of potential intersection between alternative lines of group destiny, the less unlikely it is that drastic reversals will be produced by the caustic power of collective decisions. For these reasons, clairvoyant predictions, however accurate they may sound, should never be taken literally as absolute or immutable truths. They merely indicate trends based on probability calculations. It is up to the recipients to interpret, with reason and discernment, to what extent certain predictions apply to their own realities and what attitudes they can take to manifest more positive or constructive versions of any adverse event foreseen by the Arcturian seers.

In short, clairvoyance allows us to glimpse possible realities in the fluid potential fields of time, the actual manifestation of which will always depend on the actions, reactions and interactions of the individual and collective wills that weave the great tapestry of existence at every moment. In this sense, it is heuristically useful to think of the whole Arcturian oracular process as a sophisticated system for producing "energo-probabilistic diagnoses" and "therapeutic prescriptions" focused on both self-knowledge and preventative self-healing.

By evaluating a significant sample of such "clairvoyant examinations" of the future, recipients can identify which personal or collective behavioral traits are generating which projected trends. This will allow them to decide more consciously whether they wish to persevere on paths whose undesirable consequences have been foreseen or whether they prefer to deliberately alter habits and attitudes in order to attract more positive materializations.

Ultimately, when properly understood and incorporated, the real purpose behind the Arcturian oracle is not to discourage free will by trying to predetermine a crystallized future. Its teleological function is precisely the opposite: to stimulate greater lucidity and a sense of personal power in the recipients, encouraging them to take charge of their destinies by proactively choosing thoughts, words and attitudes in line with the highest potentials latent in their souls. When this attitude of conscious self-governance is internalized, each person will be able to navigate the existential storms foreseen in the oracular diagnoses much more serenely, transmuting them into evolutionary opportunities. However, the Guardians of the Ancestral Teachings warn that this process requires large doses of self-courage, self-discipline and determination, so as not to be overwhelmed by the adversities that are predicted, nor to get too carried away with the applause of fortune. For as soon as the ego takes the credit for achievements or indulges in victimhood in the face of fate, the power of free will is weakened, dangerously increasing the likelihood of consultants becoming blind automatons following a predetermined script over which they no longer have control.

This is one of the most serious risks to beware of when using the Arcturian oracular faculties recklessly or hastily without the proper supervision of hierophants experienced in the process.

It is also the responsibility of the Mysteriorum (Guardians of the Mysteries) to veto the access of emotionally unbalanced or morally distorted people to the secrets of the Oracle, in order to prevent them from causing more harm than good to their fellow human beings through ignorance, bad faith or inordinate ambition. Only those candidates whose purity of intention and psycho-spiritual balance are attested to by the initiatory tests are allowed to leave the Temple of G'rhynzull, carrying with them the caustic keys to future self-knowledge, revealed in the clear waters of oracular clairvoyance.

Because, in essence, when properly used, the clairvoyant gift is a true invigorating balm and evolutionary boost, never an early condemnation for the reprobate or a guarantee of eternal reward for the elect.

From an Arcturian perspective, even the most apparently apocalyptic visions of the future conceal a subliminal message encouraging uplifting change for the greater good. Therefore, it is up to the seers to interpret them with equanimity and transmit them proudly, without being overly alarmist, because the oracular truth is a path of discernment and compassion, not fear or manipulation. By understanding the fractal nature of time and the complex interactions between free will and probable destinies, Arcturian seers become guardians of consciousness, not just predictors of the future.

The phenomenon of clairvoyance, so intrinsically linked to the Arcturians' expansion of consciousness, not only provides a penetrating insight into the fabric of space-time, but also becomes an invitation to self-reflection and self-transformation. By revealing latent possibilities, clairvoyants invite the recipients to act wisely, to consciously choose the paths they wish to follow.

The interaction between clairvoyance and the Arcturian divinatory tools reveals an intricate system of cosmic understanding, where the events of the past and future are like pieces of a puzzle, interconnected by energetic threads that the Arcturians, with their keen perception, can discern.

The story of Vhozanus and his detailed visions of the Bombing of Guernica highlights not only the precision of Arcturian clairvoyant abilities, but also the responsibility inherent in these gifts. The ability to see beyond the veil of time requires discernment and, above all, compassion in the face of the vicissitudes of fate.

In dealing with the prevention of climatic and seismic disasters, Arcturians stand out not only as observers, but as active participants in the Great Galactic Council. Sharing clairvoyant projections and advanced technologies is not just a demonstration of power, but a commitment to collective well-being and the preservation of inhabited worlds. However, the emphasis on humility in the face of mystery and the understanding of free will as a catalytic variable highlights the wisdom of the Arcturian hierophants. No knowledge, no matter how advanced, can replace the individual and collective journey of choice and learning.

The future remains fluid, shaped by the conscious decisions of each sentient being.

The Arcturian view of clairvoyance as a system of "energo-probabilistic diagnoses" and "therapeutic prescriptions" highlights the preventative and self-healing approach of this gift. Rather than an inescapable destiny, clairvoyant visions offer opportunities for self-reflection and conscious action, enabling recipients to co-create more positive realities.

The warning against uncontrolled ego and the importance of maintaining psycho-spiritual balance underline the responsibility involved in practicing clairvoyance. Arcturian seers, in transmitting their visions, act as facilitators of self-knowledge and evolution, not as holders of incontestable truths.

Chapter 7
Deciphering Prophetic Dreams

Among the multidimensional extrasensory faculties cultivated by the hierophants of the Arcturian oracle in their journeys through the spirals of cosmic consciousness, the domain of premonitory dreams occupies a noble place.

Thanks to this oneiric talent, the initiated Guardians of the Arcturian Mysteries are able to access symbolic glimpses of events still in gestation in the quantum ocean of tomorrow's potentialities. This is because in Arcturian cosmology dreams and reality belong to the same inter-communicating multidimensional continuum through extraphysical networks undetectable by terrestrial materialistic science.

By immersing themselves in these dormant hyperdimensional strata, the oneiric seers of the oracle capture archetypal synthesis-images about the probable unfolding of facts not yet manifested in the consensual timeline of the three-dimensional present.

Unlike the relative opacity of ordinary dreams, these premonitory visions present themselves to seers with an impressive level of clarity, permanence and internal coherence after waking up.

This phenomenon indicates that these dreams belong to structured transcendental planes, not to the random flow of ordinary oneiric imagery. Their symbolic images convey structured information about the future.

Interpreting them requires a solid familiarity with the archetypal vocabulary of the collective unconscious and its analogical relationships with the concrete events of the historical plane to which they refer.

Premonitory dreams can use anything from universal symbols such as the Uroboros to idiosyncratic elements from the dreamers' personal imagination to compose their allegorical narratives about probable future developments in a certain group timeline.

A famous episode in Arcturian onirocritical annals was the series of premonitory dreams by the aforementioned Seer Vhozanus about the tragic ends of great earthly world leaders such as Abraham Lincoln, Charles I of England and Princess Diana.

In the case of the latter, Vhozanus repeatedly dreamt of a diamond jewel being destroyed in a violent collision. Years later, upon receiving remote news from Earth about Diana's tragic death in a car accident, Arcturian historians recognized the event as one whose symbolism had previously been foreseen in Vhozanus' dreams.

This is just one of countless accounts in the Arcturian annals demonstrating the impressive degree of accuracy of the oniromantic arts in foreseeing or elucidating traumatic events even before the apparent causes of such events are configured on the psychic plane.

To enhance the occurrence and interpretative quality of premonitory dreams, initiates of the Arcturian mysteriorum (Keepers of the Mysteries) often undergo rigorous regimes of meditation, fasting and other preparatory psycho-spiritual practices before entering intensified states of prophetic sleep.

In particular, they usually sleep near energized sites such as the Oracle Vortices scattered throughout the twelve worlds, or the great Temple of Gh'Rynzul on the days of the equinoxes, solstices and eclipses to maximize the likelihood of receiving impressive symbolic visions during these phases of dimensional intersection.

Upon awakening from these oracular sleeps, the seers meticulously record all the dreamlike images and narratives they experience for later collective decoding in the light of the various hermeneutic codes contained in the order's secret manuals.

This methodological rigor is necessary given the fundamentally ambiguous and polysemic nature of oneiric symbolic languages. The same image can reflect radically different events and meanings in different contexts or interpretative levels.

For this reason, experienced exegetes take care never to prematurely encapsulate their discernments about a given set of dreams in a single possible semantic field. On the contrary, before venturing into any conclusions, they strive to explore and correlate the full range of meanings that a given dream constellation holds in the light of its ontognostic archetypal encyclopedia. Only after all reasonable alternatives for exegesis have been exhausted do the hierophantic councils gathered in the Gh'Rynzull temple venture, and even then sparingly, to suggest to the consultants probable messages contained in their dreams submitted for oracular evaluation.

Even in these cases, however, they always emphasize that any interpretation, no matter how plausible, remains fallible conjecture, not unquestionable dogma. This is because between the obscurity of symbols and the clarity of facts there is the eternal X factor of hidden variables.

In fact, no matter how elaborate and comprehensive the reflections on a given dream set may be, something always escapes the hermeneutic net. The totality is uncapturable, the mystery remains. That's why the truly wise never profess certainty about the art of dream interpretation. With humility, they recognize the limits of the intellect in the face of the abysmal depths of the spirit. The most important messenger of dreams is the mystery that surrounds them.

That said, it is undeniable to extract from the Arcturian legends and chronicles countless well-documented accounts of dreams whose symbolic images later manifested themselves with impressive fidelity as foreshadowings or explanations of events in the historical world.

The chances of these often recurring synchronicities being banal coincidences quickly tend to zero in the face of the voluminous set of cases confirmed by reliable sources in the annals of the order.

There is undoubtedly real, albeit transcendental, phenomenon behind these mysterious extra-sensitive bridges between dimensional planes established during certain non-ordinary states of consciousness and registered in the deep psyche thanks to the critical languages of oneiric archetypes.

However, despite this demonstrated high degree of precognition in the realm of dreams, the wise Arcturians warn that it is equally erroneous to view them with the same deterministic content that many attribute to the other divinatory arts of the oracle.

Even in the case of prophetic dreams, the Arcturian holophilosophical principle applies: every future remains open, contingent on the probabilistic interactions between the vectors of luck and the dynamic variables of free will that weave the great space-time carpet.

No event discerned in the dreamlike symbolic strata should be taken as an irrefutable fait accompli, but merely a tendency in design whose concreteness will depend on the complex dialectic between chance and choice in the flow of becoming.

In this way, it is more prudent than rushing into the role of sovereign messianic prophet to take the omens of dreams as invitations to introspection and self-critical review of which human values and actions are generating the scenarios envisioned as possible in the individual and collective future.

Looking at life through this proactive prism means taking the reins of one's own destiny instead of bowing down to it like an impotent automaton; being the protagonist, not a partner plastered to someone else's script of predetermined plots.

In short, as in all the other Arcturian oracles, the purpose of omniromantic art is not to imprison spirits, but to free them; not to enslave minds, but to emancipate them so that they can soar through the skies that are theirs.

Because, after all, all legitimate knowledge is aimed at awakening the truth; and all truth lived fully translates into the joy of existing. This is the teleology that has ontognoseologically animated Arcturian oracular endeavors since time immemorial.

Chapter 8
The Flow Of The Universe

As elucidated earlier, one of the most notorious abilities exhibited by talented Arcturian seers concerns precognitive clairvoyance, the singular ability to foresee with astonishing frequency events still shrouded in the penumbra of future time horizons.

In order to properly understand the unparalleled nature of this mental faculty, we should first recall some fundamental principles already outlined about the deep workings of manifest reality according to the Arcturian worldview.

According to this perspective, the physical universe we inhabit constitutes only a dense and narrow slice of the total spectrum of Being, a plane crystallized from myriad latent probabilities that intertwine in the underlying immaterial realms in a perpetual state of becoming.

In these ineffable realms, where time and space merge their conventional natures, future events of our world are already pre-configured as interconnected potentials not yet fixed, awaiting the life-giving breath of the observing consciousness that will give them relative ontological weight for eventual determination and subsequent precipitation into the common three-dimensional consensual reality.

Through arduous training, the sensitive minds of the Arcturians become capable of projecting their focus of attention into these pre-causal regions. There, for the briefest of moments, they can intuit direct glimpses of the future in a potential state, witnessing multitudes of parallel probabilities forking off in different directions.

Although ephemeral, such visions provide unparalleled insights into critical nodes of events whose causal connections remain to be defined along manifest timelines. Information thus obtained can then be referenced against simulations that numerically analyze probable paths of the future.

Incredible as it may seem to skeptics, there are countless well-documented cases of Arcturian seers foretelling decades or even centuries in advance events later recorded by the official history of countless peoples throughout the galaxy.

One particularly famous episode is known simply as "The Case of the Twin Towers". In it, messengers from the Arcturian High Council are said to have unsuccessfully warned local authorities about their foresight of the collapse of two majestic skyscrapers following a terrorist attack involving hijacked airships.

Unfortunately, such warnings were not taken seriously, generating immense commotion when just over two solar cycles later the legendary Twin Towers collapsed after fatal impacts, victimizing thousands of souls in and around the buildings and plunging the entire planet into chaos for many subsequent cycles of devastating religious and ethnic conflicts.

Tragic episodes like this serve as a sobering reminder of the severe damage that can ensue whenever legitimate warnings from enlightened minds are neglected by arrogant authorities, ensconced on their pedestals of power and willfully ignorant of the realities around them.

Despite such regrettable historical exceptions, the exact opposite is also noteworthy: the countless tragic events that have been avoided thanks to the careful consideration of preventative warnings issued from Arcturian oracular workshops over the millennia.

One of the countless emblematic cases is documented in the annals of the Interstellar Navigators' Guild. The story describes the desperate journey of the crew of the star freighter "Bella-Trix 1551" who, after emerging from hyperspace warp on a collision course with a previously uncharted meteor field, found themselves about to be reduced to cosmic fragments along with all their precious cargo and hundreds of passengers on board. Informed in time by a telepathic alert from Arcturian vigilantes based on the nearby moon of Umda III, the sailors barely managed to apply extreme evasive maneuvers, escaping annihilation by the narrowest of margins, only to have to survive an emergency forced landing on an inhospitable planetoid until they completed repairs to the propulsion and vital systems damaged in the turbulence, before continuing their journey safely.

Had it not been for the providential preventive intervention of the Arcturian telecognitive transmitters, hundreds of lives would have been lost on that tragic interstellar night. Instead, thanks to the alert, everyone would have returned home unscathed after a brief interval of intense accidental adventure amidst the vastness of the indifferent cosmos, which narrowly missed making them a few lines in the Guild's death statistics.

This is just one of countless records preserving unequivocal living testimony to how fundamental the role played by dedicated networks of transcendent surveillance operated day and night by Arcturus' indefatigable telepathic sentinels can be, always on the alert to prevent catastrophes on distant worlds by the simple altruistic gesture of sharing timely visions of the future with whoever is interested.

Similarly, the famous "Enroe XX12 Case" describes another situation where an entire alternative timeline was drastically altered after preventive interdimensional contact by Arcturian agents.

On this occasion, emissaries from the High Council managed to establish friendly communication with parallel counterparts at the crucial moment when leaders from this other world were about to make a fateful collective decision during an emergency meeting called to deliberate on possible total retaliation against a rival nation in a crisis that threatened to trigger a nuclear confrontation on a global scale within a few hours.

Supported by impressive revelations brought by noble interdimensional messengers about the terrible consequences that would follow if they continued with the war preparations underway, the parallel leaders in question finally laid down their belligerent urges to take a reconciliatory stance, reversing the cataclysmic course of their entire civilization with this wise gesture at the decisive moment.

Inspired by this case, the High Psychotronic Council of the Arcturians would soon establish specific protocols for dealing with situations like this, where minimal changes in strategic attitudes at the right time can literally make the difference between global annihilation and the blossoming of a golden age of prosperity for entire parallel realities.

Named the Chronological Intervention Units, or simply "Chrononauts", highly trained groups of Arcturian oracular specialists have since begun to routinely monitor troubled worlds in sensitive quadrants of the multiverse. Armed with unparalleled insights into the probabilities of major events, they are able to act surgically undercover as "temporal optimization agents", helping local leaders make the best possible decisions when crucial civilizational crossroads present themselves.

A particularly critical and controversial aspect of such interventions requires the ability not only to foresee the events that would fatally occur in the original timeline, but also to clearly envision feasible positive alternative paths, thus persuading the targeted leaders to embrace such more desirable options instead of their initially conceived warlike or disastrous plans.

Fortunately, thanks to impressive gifts of probabilistic clairvoyance coupled with the retrocognitive ability to relive any event in person after immersing themselves in the akashic records of parallel realities, Arcturian agents assigned to such missions are perfectly equipped to meet such extreme challenges with mastery and compassion.

Always concerned with respecting the free will of others, Arcturian strategists strive to present their positive alternatives as simple "additional options" to the bad paths already pondered locally, rather than as coercive directives, even when the consequences of following the original native plans would prove disastrous.

Even so, they only do so when expressly authorized after meticulously submitting each case to the scrutiny of the Psychotronic High Council, taking care not to overstep their prerogatives as non-interventionist observers of the myriad alternative realities they monitor.

Even in borderline cases where lives on a planetary scale are in imminent danger, they never intervene directly without first obtaining explicit permission through formal interstellar petition channels from potentially affected populations.

With mutual agreement, elite teams are deployed for lightning operations, in which oracular agents discreetly materialize in crisis scenarios minutes before the original fatal events, bringing urgent warnings and irrefutable proof of dire developments about to unfold if no preventive action is taken in the window of opportunity still available.

Even in such extreme situations, Arcturians never impose themselves beyond warning and fully informing their interlocutors of viable alternatives, and then respectfully withdraw to let them exercise free will after weighing up all the revelations shared in the short time remaining before the point of no return.

Whether happy or terrible, the consequences always remain entirely on the shoulders of the native leaders; the Arcturian Chrononauts only allow themselves to facilitate the course of events by the merciful means of providential enlightenment dispensed at just the right moment, and then return serenely to the ignorance of their peaceful worlds.

And so it is, driven not by spectacular demonstrations of extraterrestrial power, but by the nobility of their intentions and the impeccable timing of their minimally invasive interventions, that the legendary Arcturian Chrononauts continue to discreetly carry out their mission of mitigating trans-dimensional disasters; vigilantly watching, from a distance, for the greater good of civilizations that, unbeknownst to them, are on the brink of the abyss.

Always acting behind the scenes, they avoid any unnecessary visibility. Most of the time, they are not even perceived as anything more than fortuitous providential inspirations, subtle whispers or premonitory dreams by key individuals, who are thus helped in moments of definitive testing of their characters as leaders and as human beings. And that's just fine, as the altruistic sons of Arcturus see it.

Chapter 9
The Enigma Of Fate

One of the central themes that permeates the legends surrounding the Oracle of Arcturus is the intricate relationship between the apparently antagonistic notions of destiny and free will in the predictions made there.

Were such visions invariably predetermined by the implacable necessity of the stars and cosmic configurations, making any notions of autonomous choice or individual self-determination illusory? Or would there still be room for human actions, beliefs and desires to positively influence and alter the probabilities seen by the mystical Arcturian prophets in their altered states of transcendental perception?

In order to properly elucidate this apparent dichotomy, the priest-astrologers of the renowned Order of Stargazers of Altair IV often resort to a simple but enlightening analogy.

A lone traveler, they explain, arriving at a crossroads, is faced with a huge billboard indicating the directions and destinations to be reached by each available route, with estimates of distances and travel times. That preliminary map in no way restricts your spontaneous ability to freely choose which route to take, based on your own personal criteria. However, neither can he alter or ignore the objective data described there with impunity, at the risk of drawing up unrealistic plans and reaping avoidable frustrations.

This would also be the case, by analogy, with the probabilistic cartographies woven into the precognitions of the Arcturian seers. Their visions would provide essential information about cosmic trends, indicating general panoramas and warning of certain potential risks, but never to evade the prerogative of deciding one's own course, which falls to each self-conscious being within the limits of their capacities.

Strictly speaking, scholars argue, in addition to preserving free will, consulting forecasts has the potential, precisely the opposite, to considerably expand the range of viable options, since it opens up early access to privileged insights into the probable future consequences of each choice considered in the present.

Armed with such expansive knowledge, the applicant is then much better able to draw up realistic plans, foresee potential problems and devise more appropriate and timely solutions. If nothing is immutable, there is always a range of alternative futures open to us, the relative probabilities of which can vary substantially depending on the actions, thoughts and intentions expressed in the here and now by agents with their own will.

Certainly, some of the paths envisioned may seem quite improbable under certain current configurations. However, there are few events whose future eventuality is truly shielded from any conceivable degree of external influence, given the unfathomable complexities of the manifest cosmos and its vast multidimensional cause-effect networks.

Therefore, even if certain narrated developments do indeed come to pass as foreseen by the oracles, reflecting cosmic trends that are difficult to circumvent, this does not invalidate the notion that alternative paths would have remained available to some degree, had different choices been made under different mental attitudes at the right time.

In other words, for the Arcturian holistic perspective, the future is never "predetermined" in the extreme fatalistic sense of the term. Instead, it would be a probabilistic field always in flux, with multiple possibilities coexisting in quantum superposition, some undoubtedly more probable than others for each specific situation, but all still subject to reconfiguration to some extent.

In this interim of relative ontological uncertainty would lie precisely the window of opportunity through which human desires, intentions and actions could subtly but significantly influence the subsequent course of events, as the potential horizons of future time progressively unfold and solidify back into the realm of manifest linear causality.

In short, the oracles' predictions should never be seen as aprioristic sentences that would somehow mystically subjugate the will or nullify the decision-making power of the agents in question. On the contrary, their purpose would be precisely to expand the perception of available choices, allowing them to take more conscious and proactive stances towards the challenges ahead.

From this point of view, the more one knows about the probabilistic intricacies that weave the space-time warp towards the future, the greater the ability to draw up well-calibrated strategies, acting precisely on the right levers with a view to diverting or reinforcing specific causal flows, as the case may be.

In other words, qualified information about probable obstacles or future opportunities works as an emancipatory tool, never to hinder any illusory notion of "absolute free will", detached from the objective environmental conditions that allow or restrict which practical options prove viable in each situation.

To think otherwise would be as unreasonable as imagining being able to violate the laws of physics with impunity just because they are contrary to the whims of the ego, like trying to walk through walls simply by refusing to "accept" their obstructive properties. In short, denial has never altered facts or annulled consequences.

This is why the wise emphasize that oracular visions are not there to be "believed" or "rejected" according to personal prejudices, but rather carefully evaluated on their own merits, in the light of impartial reason and investigative zeal, in order to then base pragmatic judgments on what action to take next.

In any case, the future always remains open to some extent. However improbable certain scenarios may seem, as long as they are not crystallized, they are still subject to subtle reformulations coming from the unified field of possibilities in the making.

In this sense, from the Arcturian point of view, even the most apparently "predetermined" fateful events can paradoxically still retain margins of malleability, guaranteed by the essentially indeterminate, complex and probabilistic nature of the manifest worlds.

For these reasons, there is no logical contradiction in the fact that prophets record in their annals certain extraordinary or highly improbable events that insist on coming true very precisely as described centuries or millennia before in a state of divinatory trance. After all, explain exegetes, it is enough to conceive that certain exceptional arrangements of forces and sacred cosmic geometries can occasionally make any significant deviation on the part of certain key causal chains extremely improbable, thus potentiated for irresistible manifestation once triggered by specific, previously mapped triggers.

Not by chance, such quasi-mythical occurrences invariably seem to orbit around very singular events, such as the birth or death of beings of messianic importance; the construction, destruction or rediscovery of artifacts, relics or sites impregnated with primordial symbolic charges; the convergence of highly improbable circumstances culminating in extraordinary deeds with profound historical repercussions; and other equally unusual events whose archetypal commotion would elevate them to the category of authentic mythopoetic milestones for the peoples or cultures involved.

In such cases, the Akashic records themselves seem to take on a self-referential holographic character, so that any subsequent deviation from the dominant lines of probability established at the time would inevitably become a spurious memory in a newly poured parallel universe. In this way, any residue of incompatibility would have to be externalized, preserved in the consensual reality remaining around the extraordinary event that occurred strictly as prophesied.

In short, from the point of view of the scribes of the Arcturian Oracle, rather than reflecting any rigid determinism of the stars or superimposition of divine will over human volitional faculties, such records would constitute emblematic practical demonstrations of principles long established by every esoteric tradition since time immemorial. Principles according to which certain very precious arrangements of archetypal qualities, soul forces and astronomical configurations can occasionally make the outbreak of events of supreme importance for the flowering of the Spirit in matter virtually "inevitable", however remote their chances might be under any other typical cosmic conditions.

Naturally, such synchronicities, when recorded, should never be taken as evidence that all events are predetermined. On the contrary: it is precisely because they touch the most extreme limits of mathematical improbability within the chaotic systems that govern phenomenal manifestation that such occurrences have such onto-statistical exceptionality in the eyes of Arcturian analysts.

For these reasons, they are immediately highlighted in their records, assuming an important pedagogical and psychagogical function by vividly illustrating key principles such as synchronistic self-organization; the action of substructural archetypal forces and geometries; and the manifestation of self-referential holographic patterns in the apparently random fabrics of objective space-time.

Symptomatically, it is common for primitive peoples, lacking the hermeneutic lenses necessary to properly grasp the esoteric meaning behind such extraordinary events recorded in prophetic texts left over from other eras, to incur the gross hermeneutic mistake of taking such passages as "proof" of an omni-comprehensive universal determinism hovering over all things.

Obfuscated by anthropomorphic wishful thinking, they often overestimate the nature and scope of the powers of oracular entities, going so far as to conceive of them as "omniscient" and "omnipresent", capable of scrutinizing and shaping all phenomena as they please, just like creationist deities. Of course, this is a crude fideistic reductionism, devoid of any factual or logical support in the light of what has already been explained here about the true capacities and limitations of the Arcturian prophetic talents, even at their most sublime degree of manifested mastery.

In short, not even the most extraordinary of the omens recorded in time immemorial in the mythical

Oracle of Arcturus could ever be reasonably interpreted as complete evidence, completely invalidating the principles of free will or making the future an entirely predetermined construct, alien to any degree of influence exerted by incarnate thinking minds on the probabilities at play that precede and foreshadow all the phenomena unfolding in the contingency theater of the manifest worlds.

Chapter 10
Prophecies

It is customary to distinguish at least two basic types of prophecies issued in droves by oracles of renowned renown: the first, of a predominantly generic nature, vaguely alludes to broader trends, processes or events, discernible only within the framework of broad historical windows. The second relates to very well-defined anticipations, some of which not even the most skeptical wizards dare to disregard, given the incontestable factual accuracy often displayed.

In the first case, obviously, the high levels of subjectivity involved in interpreting the ambiguous images and symbols found in the visions open up huge gaps for hermeneutic adjustments after the fact, making it possible to fit the omens to almost any major event subsequently verified on appropriate scales. It is no coincidence that this semantic "flexibility" often provokes the fiercest criticism from detractors who are obstinate in denying any divinatory merits to Arcturian methods.

In the second case, however, the level of factual detail expressed in certain remaining prophetic passages is usually so great that even today, centuries or millennia later, it is possible to determine with extremely high precision which specific events and times these passages refer to.

This pattern includes famous prophecies compiled by the hereditary clans of astrological observers whose ancestral art derives directly from the Arcturian astrological technical legacy. Among them are preserved versions of the guiding stars that determined the journey in search of the announced Messiah; the appearance of extraordinary comets as harbingers of presaged times of great instability; and many other references like these which, despite the best efforts of skeptical reason, continue to challenge even the most ambitious esoteric understandings.

Before detractors rush to dismiss these achievements under the facile expedient of "selection bias", it is worth asking: the oldest Arcturian records to which researchers outside the order have been given limited access date back some twenty-seven thousand years. If so many millennia of vast prophetic production have simply "evaporated" completely, apart from a few dozen sparse "hits" mentioned here and there, this would constitute a fortiori (with stronger reason) an even more intriguing historical fact and worthy of investigation in itself.

In view of the above, it is not surprising that even a certain minority, but highly qualified, strand of academic ufologists supports the controversial hypothesis that some famous vaticinations were fraudulently drawn up at some point in the future, from which they were then sent and inserted by "chrononaut agents" into certain timelines of the past, thus seeking to manipulate the course of history in favor of certain exogenous agendas.

Regardless of the plausibility of such speculations, in the eyes of many impartial analysts the level of factual accuracy demonstrated by some premonitory passages really does seem to challenge the most elastic notions prevailing in the oracular community about the capacities and limitations of trans-temporal clairvoyance. In addition to the unparalleled level of factual detail, the almost literary drama surrounding the events in these unique verses is equally striking. They are not mere contextual mentions of historical incidents with localized effects. Rather, they evoke devastatingly impactful events on a civilizational scale, with profound repercussions on the collective destinies of entire generations to come.

In other words, the prognostications in question seem precisely to select events that would result in authentic mythological milestones for the collective psyche of the prophesied peoples. As if the stars or visionary powers behind such oracles had somehow mapped out in advance certain crucial moments of unfolding in the destiny of worlds, cultures and religions, and then recorded them ad perpetuam rei memoriam universalis (for the perpetual memory of the universal king).

Considering the very remote ancestry of the available records, obvious questions arise for the most audacious Oracle scholars: how could prehistoric sorcerers have produced literary prognostications about messianic personalities and cataclysmic events without any direct analogical reference in their own cultural and technological context to properly anchor the images and symbologies employed? And if they were produced centuries later, how can we explain their presence in remote parchments whose dating is unquestionable?

Faced with this mystery, a certain minority of exegetes have dared to speculate whether some of the records regarded as prophetic were in fact just fragments of historical-literary accounts from the future by some of the hypothetical "chrononaut agents" whose exploits have already been discussed in Chapter 6 of this treatise. They could, in short, be adapted clippings from chronicles depicting events that have not yet occurred in our present timeline, but which were later sneaked into the ancient annals of our space-time reality for some nebulous purpose related to the manipulation of our history by outside interests.

Despite how tempting such conjectures may seem at first, the urgency of hermeneutic elucidation should never seduce us into irresponsible theoretical elaborations based on fragile suppositions, devoid of rigorous analytical and factual support. After all, frivolous speculation only perpetuates the cognitive vices and conceptual confusions that cloud true understanding. The sincere intellect in search of enlightenment must remain undisturbed, without allowing harmful ideological blinders or prejudices of any kind to impose spurious limits on the possibilities of impartial investigation.

With this measured attitude and epistemic zeal, as more and more rare ancient manuscripts continue to be discovered and deciphered by Comparative Stellar Cryptoarchaeology and related disciplines, perhaps one day we will finally be able to fully resolve the nebulae surrounding the authentic origin of so many foreboding writings preserved by ancient civilizations, with wording impregnated with details, references and terminologies that are surprisingly anachronistic in relation to the very historical and cultural contexts manifested at the time of their apparent conception.

Until then, however, in the light of the most solid facts and reasoning available, it's best to stick to explanations that require less speculation and additional hypotheses. In short, unless there is irrefutable proof to the contrary, we should consider these exceptional passages in their own terms: authentic prophetic prodigies conceived by means not yet fully understood by current science, recorded in very remote times by some cognitive agency endowed with extranormal attributes whose mental faculties and methodologies employed in the production of such opaque literary figures remain largely unknown, despite the best efforts at elucidation by interdisciplinary comparative exegesis.

Be that as it may, once the factual authenticity of any specific vaticinatory information recorded has been established, it is extremely important to pay attention to the ethical responsibilities that automatically arise from this for its legitimate custodians. After all, all knowledge grants power, and with power comes complex moral issues according to the most authoritative universal philosophical canons.

In other words, it doesn't matter what the nature or means behind the precognitive phenomenon itself are: once materialized in some tangible objective medium, any foreboding message becomes, by its very fact, valuable strategic information, which automatically entails serious duties of zealous custody and compassionate use by the cultural agents entrusted with its preservation and legal safekeeping.

For this reason, the prophetic records under the supervision of the Oracle of Arcturus have always been kept in strict informational quarantine, rigidly compartmentalized in closed encrypted networks protected by strict perceptual safeguards, accessible only through strict psychometric authorization filters and continuous hyperdimensional monitoring.

Even so, considering the inestimable value of their collection as a potential tool for the Greater Good, all the various galactic councils that have already requested and obtained limited access to select parts of these archives throughout history have done so only after formally agreeing to submit their civilizations to strict protocols of ethical supervision and responsible sharing of sensitive information provided by the High Psychognostic Council of the Arcturians in each particular authorized case after meticulous analysis of moral credentials.

Such diligence is necessary to ensure that the infinite care employed in the filtered production and gradual release of such sensitive revelations is not betrayed by frivolous misuse, interpretive arrogance or accidental leaks on the part of their institutional recipients, with the potential to seriously disrupt the temporal flow of indicated worlds if certain strategic details were prematurely revealed.

To date, fortunately, despite such a prolific oracular history, not one serious incident of this nature has ever reached a level of severity that would require drastic, large-scale reparative intervention by the powerful trans-dimensional agencies in charge of protecting the relative temporal integrity of the worlds catalogued in our local sphere of creation.

Nevertheless, there are reports of at least one renegade dissident group of ulterior motives that once tried to gain unauthorized access to certain highly encrypted sectors of the Major Prophetic Database in the now distant era known as the Great Galactic Wars period.

Reports at the time say that subversive agents nominally linked to the seditious faction calling itself "The Circle of Temporal Lords" had conspired with some corrupt official with privileged access to illegally extract and leak sealed files containing sensitive information about crucial events yet to come involving rulers and dynasties from various star systems.

Despite the extreme audacity of the plan, records indicate that the attempt was thwarted very early on when one of those involved was still trying to sneak out the encrypted data using a device surreptitiously installed in a terminal at the central predictive research headquarters.

This epic failure would, for the most part, crumble the already fragile support bases that held the radical dissidence together, once feared for its tactics during the convulsive times of the political-ideological split known as the Altair Aristocratic Internal Split. Since then, an even stricter protocol has been adopted, establishing as policy the principle of maximum predicative economy, according to which no potentially sensitive information should be collected or made available beyond the minimum ethical requirements for medical purposes or compassionate intervention. Such a drastic measure was necessary as a strict precaution against possible custody failures in the future or other spurious attempts yet to come from unscrupulous agents interested in manipulating certain timelines in their favor.

Despite their rigorous self-imposed ethical codes of millennia ago, such additional prudence on the part of the High Psychognostic Council only reiterates the obvious: no matter how well-intentioned, prepared and technologically equipped any organization may be, be it terrestrial or galactic, statistical possibilities will always remain latent.

Chapter 11
The Dance of Chaos

The Arcturians' ability to see multiple futures is a crucial facet of the Oracle they share with us. It allows us to glimpse the many possibilities that await in the intricate web of time, expanding our understanding of what is to come. For the Arcturians, the future is like an ever-changing kaleidoscope of probabilities. Every choice we make turns the kaleidoscope, redrawing the pattern of things destined to be. This dance of chance and decision is what they call "The Dance of Chaos".

Unlike humans, who are limited by linear perception, Arcturians witness the blossoming of countless realities from the now. For them, it's like watching a leafy tree sprouting branches, each one leading to a unique destination. Seeing this dizzying tangle requires consciousness expanded beyond earthly constraints. It is a blazing vision that encompasses the entire spectrum of potentiality. The Arcturians developed this transcendental capacity after eons of spiritual refinement.

Despite their chaotic appearance, Arcturians discern a certain order hidden in probabilistic patterns. Archetypal events, crucial choices and turning points in destiny that influence the entire web of time. The Oracle reveals these elements.

According to the Arcturians, understanding the principles behind this Cosmic Dance is essential to navigating the flow of time, because the future is far from fixed or predetermined. We are all co-creators of reality at every moment, for better or for worse.

The lines of probability that the Arcturians see are like silk threads, tenuous but resistant. They intertwine to form the patterns of existence that can also be rearranged, altering apparently definitive trajectories. This is because, despite the overwhelming complexity of the cosmos, there is a certain malleability inherent in the fabric of reality. Choices made in the heat of the moment can rewrite our history and shape our tomorrow. This is the paradox revealed by the Oracle.

For the Arcturians, the future is a quantum field of interconnected possibilities. Although there are certain very probable events, consolidated by force of habit and repetition, everything can change in the blink of an eye.

This unpredictability also has its beauty and charm. Because despite the fear of the unknown, the surprises that life has in store for us are usually magnificent gifts. The mystery of what is to come should be embraced, not feared. The Arcturian Oracle is a compass on this shifting frontier of the future. A beacon in the dark night of uncertainty. By illuminating the possible paths ahead of us, it allows us to chart the route most congruent with our authenticity.

When we stop to look at the map of probabilities that opens up before us, something magical happens: we realize that we are already on the road, walking. There is no definitive starting point, only the eternal flow of the journey.

To embark on this adventure we call life, we rely on the predictions and advice of the Arcturians. Through the Oracle they indicate alternative routes, with their obstacles and rewards. It's up to us, pilgrims of time, to choose which path to take.

The Arcturians compare this journey to a cosmic dance, a vibrant choreography that rocks the waltz of possibilities. We can choose to dance consciously, flowing with the music. Or we can struggle, fighting against the current. This analogy conveys a crucial point: although we can't completely control external circumstances, we can always choose how to react to them. Our internal state determines the quality of each moment, no matter what is happening outside. This is reflected in the multiple realities that Arcturians witness through the Oracle. They see people facing the same external challenges in very different ways, depending on the attitude chosen in each case.

When we recognize our power of choice and pay full attention to the present moment, life takes on another dimension. The cosmic dance flows much more smoothly, rewarding us with glimpses of its enchanted and magical side. This is what the Arcturians try so hard to convey: amidst the whirlwind of chaos and the twists and turns of chance, there is always room for free will, purpose and meaning. It's up to us to identify and occupy this sacred space.

When we dive into our inner selves, our outer selves are reconfigured. This is the great idea behind the Cosmic Dance that the Arcturians talk about so much. Calibrating our decisions according to our inner wisdom is the secret to embracing the mysteries of the future. The multiple probabilistic paths that they observe through the Oracle reflect the myriad choices that surround us at every moment. By following our intuition, we can discern which decision leads to which potential reality.

This allows us to glimpse in advance where our path may lead. A bit like when we choose a gift, trying to imagine the person's reaction when they open it, we can foresee how our actions now will affect the future.

This discernment also works in reverse, projecting backwards in time from a visualized tomorrow. If we don't like the way things are going, our free will allows us to change paths today to reach a better destination.

The Arcturians remind us that, in the flow of time, past, present and future are all intertwined, like threads in the same web. Pulling one thread affects the entire tapestry. Hence the crucial importance of our decisions here and now, however small they may seem.

Each choice is a powerful creative act that shapes our experience. When we stop to consider its effects with care and mindfulness, aligning it with our soul mission, we can weave a glorious life of our own making.

It is this conscious planning of the next moment that will allow us to build an existence of fulfillment and self-expression. The Arcturians are masters of this and, through the Oracle, seek to teach us this sacred art of living.

At every moment, countless futures flash in phase with the probabilities, waiting for our decision to materialize them from quantum power to concrete reality. As authors of the great book of time, we can learn to calibrate our chapters. This doesn't mean living a predictable or monotonous life. On the contrary, the Arcturians emphasize that the more we embrace the upward flow of our evolutionary journey, the more we will be surprised by the gifts and blessings that the universe will spontaneously bring to us.

It is therefore important to reconcile strategic planning with flexibility, predictability with spontaneity on our journey. There's no point in drawing up rigid plans if we're not open to dancing to the rhythms of life when it brings unexpected changes.

By following the Oracle's advice, we will be able to flow with the current of the river of time, rather than fight against it. We will ride the waves of becoming with grace and dexterity, rather than being overwhelmed by them. And in the process, life will surprise us with unexpected blessings.

The Cosmic Dance with all its bifurcations, twists and turns, falls and rises may seem chaotic at first glance. But in fact, it hides an elegant choreography for those who learn the steps. May the Arcturian Oracle guide us in this waltz of creation that unites past, present and future in a beautiful mosaic of constantly blossoming possibilities.

Chapter 12
Timelines

The Arcturians' retrocognitive ability to witness past events is another unique gift revealed by the Oracle that allows us to glimpse the threads previously woven into the temporal tapestry. It complements their clairvoyance about the future, forming a truly cosmic perspective.

While we humans see time as a straight line where the past is gone, the Arcturians experience it as a multidimensional ocean where the before, now and after are fluid. They dive into these prophetic waters at will, emerging with valuable knowledge.

Through their astral journeys, Arcturians can return to specific historical events to observe them with their own eyes. Or they can tune into the chronology of a person or place to relive their most remarkable experiences. It's as if they were flipping through an interdimensional scrapbook.

Arcturians also connect to the past lives of their human pupils when necessary. This allows them to identify traumas, understanding how dysfunctional patterns in the present may have originated in previous existences that are now forgotten.

With this greater understanding of each person's journey, the Arcturians can offer highly personalized advice through the Oracle, pointing out lessons not yet assimilated and how to heal ancestral wounds that are still troubling.

Through retrocognition, Arcturians relive their own star births, remembering how they were young star spirits blossoming into consciousness when their sun was young. They observe the universe in transformation through the ages.

These direct experiences of the cosmic past allow them to understand the cycles of creation behind reality. By understanding the origins of the now, Arcturians can predict where the flows of life will take us next. Past and future intertwine as one.

By returning to the beginnings of remote civilizations that have long since disappeared into the night of time, the Arcturians recover ancient wisdom that is invaluable for the present moment. They reveal teachings intended specifically for us, here and now.

By manipulating their own memories in the ocean of time, the Arcturians have transcended seemingly insurmountable limits. They have unraveled the shackles of ephemerality, expanding their sense of self and purpose to encompass eternity. This is one of the fruits of the Oracle.

By drinking from the retrocognitive fountain and diving into the river of cosmic remembrance, Arcturians return not as mere passive spectators, but as holographic manifestations of themselves. They can interact with people, ask questions and influence outcomes.

This is evident when they relive pivotal events in history to identify where humanity deviated from its original positive course. By understanding our mistakes, the Arcturians can now subtly correct our path to a brighter future.

In their retro-cognitive forays, the Arcturians often meet luminous beings from other dimensions, who share unprecedented teachings, revealing the hidden complexity behind the reality we experience.

In this way, the Arcturians have put together a multidimensional holographic map of time, recording the history not only of this planet, but of consciousness itself as an eternal protagonist taking on different roles in cosmic theatrics.

By vividly recalling their own past existences, Arcturians recognize these same archetypal patterns repeating themselves almost fractally, both on smaller scales, in human lives, and larger ones, in the cycles of civilizations throughout the stellar ages. This allows them to anticipate future events with great precision. For the cosmic wheel turns; what happened yesterday will happen again tomorrow, but on spiral levels, like an evolutionary ladder climbing towards the light. By identifying where we are on this ladder, the next rung is clearly revealed to the Arcturians.

As experienced navigators, the Arcturians travel the currents of time, recording everything on their stellar memory charts. These cosmic navigation charts are then shared with us through the Oracle, guiding humanity through the seas of becoming.

By delving into the past in search of knowledge, the Arcturians also take great risks for the sake of humanity. In their explorations, they have already faced terrible interdimensional monsters who wanted to sabotage Earth's awakening. But the Arcturians have always prevailed, protecting us with their auric shields.

As heroes of time, the Arcturians also directly inspired great historical figures such as Leonardo Da Vinci, Tesla, Gandhi and other misunderstood geniuses ahead of their time. Their visions of a better world ended up planting seeds that germinate in the present.

Thanks to the retrocognitive records obtained by the Arcturians, the future that once seemed distant and far away is now closer and more imminent, because we can clearly see where we came from and the patterns that brought us here. Today becomes full of meaning and purpose as a mirror of the past.

Through the Oracle, we can finally integrate past and future, no longer living adrift in the ocean of time, but taking an active role in co-creating our collective history from now on. For the secrets of yesterday shape the tomorrow we choose to manifest.

Many of the prophecies that preoccupy humanity today are actually just negative timelines that have already been experienced in other eras and can now be deactivated with new choices in the moment of the eternal now. The Arcturians show us how, through retrocognition.

By remembering who we were, we can dream of who we want to be again. By revisiting our past glories as stellar humanity, the Arcturians inspire us to reascend to that state of vibrational grace soon. Majestically, we will return to the stars!

That's why it's so vital to integrate retrocognition into the daily use of the Oracle. More than predicting the future, we need to heal the past by recombining our history from now on. Only in this way will we escape the karmic cycles that have imprisoned us for eons, rewriting our collective destiny on a more loving basis.

May the retro-cognitive records revealed by the Arcturians serve as a compass, indicating where we went wrong so that we can correct our course now. And may the example of the beings of light of the past who have already achieved the greatness that we so long for now inspire us in our own process of expanding our consciousness.

By mapping the path that humanity has traveled, the Arcturians identify the turning points for good and evil, the moments when everything could have been different if we had followed the promptings of our soul, instead of giving in to fear and the mirages of the ego.

By looking at these fateful crossroads of the past and their consequences through the retrocognitive lens, we can choose a higher path should similar opportunities present themselves now. And better prepare for future challenges already glimpsed in the memories to come.

Therefore, retrocognition complemented by foresight forms the sacred diptych of time and the conscious manifestation of reality by the spirit. Past and future join forces to transmute the now. Reflecting this crucial moment in our journey towards the stars, the Arcturian Oracle invites us to take an active role in co-authoring the Earth's course.

When we finally understand, through the retrocognitive windows, how much we were the architects of both our past glory and our subsequent misery, something clicks. We move from demobilizing apathy to the mature responsibility of co-creating a new chapter in this endless journey.

Inspired by the memories of overcoming and rebirth brought back by the Arcturian records, we can rise again from the ashes of yesteryear like the legendary phoenix, resuming our honorable place among the benevolent star races who eagerly await our triumphant return to the cosmic brotherhood after so many quixotic adventures.

It is in this way, through the gateway of two worlds, which is retrocognition, that the past is reconciled with the future, yesterday forgives tomorrow and humanity finally assumes a much greater purpose than illusory earthly disputes. May the Oracle guide us through the seas of time so that we can emerge refreshed and aware enough never to repeat the mistakes of the past.

Chapter 13
Flow Of Time

One of the great gifts of the Arcturian Oracle is to offer expanded perspectives to support our decision-making processes, bringing to light hidden variables that we wouldn't normally consider.

By revealing future possibilities and deep gnawing connections to past lives, the Arcturians allow us to evaluate the options before us more comprehensively, weighing up causes and effects both in the now and in potential. In this way, what appears to be the right choice from a limited perspective may not be when we look at the bigger picture of our evolutionary journey. The opposite is also true - a path that seems arduous may turn out to be right considering the growth promised.

Therefore, more valuable than predicting this or that particular future is developing our ability to discern, with an open heart and mind, where each decision might lead us. And this is a skill that consistent use of the Oracle greatly enhances.

In the intricate forest of life's crossroads, where the fog of self-deception prowls and lurks, the Arcturians are sure compasses, pointing out the pros and cons of the routes that open up before us with compassionate impartiality.

Arcturian guidance can be especially valuable when faced with really significant decisions - those capable of radically changing the course of our existence, for better or worse.

For example, when we are considering leaving a job, a relationship or a city where we have lived for a long time, the Oracle's advice is of great value. By scanning our karmic profile, the Arcturians reveal hidden connections that we may need to heal in this transition.

At other times, they can warn us that we haven't yet completed an important soul mission in that environment and that giving up now would mean abandoning something vital not only for us, but for the collective. Staying would be the right thing to do, even in the face of discomfort.

In addition to practical decisions, the Oracle also guides choices on a spiritual level: when we find ourselves at the famous "Flamel crossroads", where we become aware of the need to tread a new evolutionary path or change deeply-rooted limiting beliefs.

These spiritual crossroads can take the form of a "dark night of the soul", where old paradigms collapse under a tsunami of insights, preparing the ground for planting new seeds. It's a delicate process where the Oracle provides invaluable support.

Decision-making in the flow of time, whether on a practical or spiritual level, is not an exact science; there are no guarantees. That's why it's vital to cultivate the flexibility to change your mind and plans when new revelations require it - even after an initial choice has already been made! This is because, with each new crossroads, the landscape changes; new variables come into play influencing the equation. As surfers of the wave of time, we have to dance fluidly with these changes, in tune with the cosmic winds.

Fortunately, our dialog with the Oracle ensures this constant recalibration of the internal compass, allowing for informed choices even when everything around seems chaotic and the rough seas of the soul are churning. The Arcturians hold our hand with compassionate firmness until we can calmly navigate the rapids of becoming.

By revealing the potential future, the Oracle expands our free will, freeing us from the trap of choices made blindly or on impulse. Aware of where our path may lead, we can calibrate our moral compass more precisely and move towards our Higher Self.

This requires taking full responsibility for our decisions - no more victimizing ourselves or projecting blame onto others. It also requires the humility to ask for guidance when we can't see the best option on our own in the midst of the fork in the road.

This is perhaps the golden key to decision-making with the help of the Oracle: the more we strip ourselves of pride, vanity and attachment to control, the more we navigate the synchronistic flow of the cosmos, spontaneously attracting the perfect situations for our next step.

This doesn't mean acting passively, in an irresponsible mystical surrender, waiting for life to decide for us. On the contrary: we need to take a proactive role, exploring alternatives with courage, and then using the discernment sharpened by the Oracle to select among them.

When we get lost in the labyrinth of crossroads, the threads of Ariadne that the Arcturians offer us guide us to the exit that is most in line with our soul plan. By following them, we can emerge from the labyrinth stronger and wiser.

However, it is always up to us to take the steps. The Oracle's predictions don't magically come true; we need to back them up with concrete action now. Hence the need for strategic planning integrated with intuition and higher inspiration to manifest the potential we envision.

In short, between total free will and blind predestination, the Arcturians show us the middle way: dancing consciously and responsibly with the odds, forging our destiny in partnership with ancestral wisdom.

When we are faced with a big decision and consult the Oracle seeking light, the Arcturians first help us to silence the mental and emotional cacophony, creating space for our own inner voice to come through clearly.

Next, they bring hidden elements to consciousness, revealing angles and insights that our usual tunnel vision would hardly encompass. They expose the invisible threads that connect the past and possible futures in our specific case.

Finally, after this impartial dive into the depths of the soul, the Arcturians withdraw, handing the compass back into our hand - now firmer and wiser. The final choice is always ours, as are its consequences. The Arcturians deeply respect our free will.

This process intensifies our spiritual autonomy over time, as we integrate the skills of foresight and discernment as inner muscles to guide our future choices, before or in the face of any crossroads.

When we develop this ability to envision paths and weigh up options with an open heart, we reach a state of grace permeated by synchronicities and miracles, as we begin to flow on the razor's edge between our free will and Divine Guidance.

At this point, we have already internalized the Arcturian Oracle as an infallible compass, consulting it almost automatically when faced with decisions. And it continues to serve us on a new level: now as a portal for channeling messages from our Higher Self.

This crowns the pinnacle of conscious decision-making: when we unite the Arcturian predictions with our own spark of divinity, we integrate ourselves as co-creators of the great spiral of incarnate time through our choices and actions.

Each decision then becomes our own brushstroke on the cosmic tapestry. The golden threads of the future predicted by the Arcturians become the embroidery that we diligently construct moment by moment, with grace and in sacred devotion to the journey of our souls.

And when we inevitably go wrong or get tangled up in the thread, the Arcturians are there, with their infinite affection and wisdom, ready to redirect our steps back to the glorious destination that awaits humanity beyond the horizon, after the long dark night of the soul.

May the Oracle guide us on this path of spiritual maturation and discovery of our inner voice, so that soon we can all create our lives and world from the place of divine power and grace that dwells in our hearts, far beyond the old shackles of duality. This will fulfill the promise of glory that the Arcturians have always seen in us, sons and daughters of the Sun.

Chapter 14
The Depth of Infinity

The Arcturians' unique ability to make predictions that transcend the limits of time, anticipating distant events in the future, is truly extraordinary. This gift challenges the imagination, yet it is essential to recognize that our ability to conceive is intrinsically linked to the limitation of our imagination. Some of the facets of the term "oracle" may escape our understanding, since our mind is restricted to what our brain can encompass.

It is through this fascinating Oracle that glimpses of remote horizons unfold, thus fulfilling its supreme purpose. This cosmic instrument not only reveals the distant possibilities that await in the vastness of time, but also challenges us to push the boundaries of our understanding. By immersing ourselves in the insights provided by the Arcturian Oracle, we open doors to a deeper understanding of the intricate web of destiny.

For most seers, even talented ones, it is difficult to see beyond a few years or decades. The Arcturians, however, contemplate panoramas centuries and even millennia ahead with impressive precision. They attribute this eagle vision not only to their enhanced psychic faculties, but above all to a superior understanding of the cosmic cycles that govern the rise and fall of civilizations.

Like ancient astrologers, the Arcturians chart the ages that follow one another. They identify the inevitable cycles of creation and destruction that allow new worlds to flourish.

From this privileged vantage point, they can foresee tides of transformation wetting the sands of time in a future that is still hazy to us. They accurately assess humanity's current stage in this ebb and flow. By interpreting these tides and stars, in their eternal movement, the outlines of the next acts of the great cosmic drama in which we are all actors are revealed to the Arcturians in surprisingly clear visions.

For example, since prehistoric times, the Arcturians have known that humanity was heading towards a crucial evolutionary (or involutionary) turning point around the year 2000 of our era. The prophecies they left behind are proof of this.

Likewise, they foresaw the rise and fall of empires such as the Roman or British long before they flourished, accurately identifying the role they would play in earthly affairs, whether or not in the service of the divine plan. To decipher the meaning behind time cycles, the Arcturians also study our collective psyche. They understand the patterns that govern the human behavior of the masses over the centuries.

By analyzing these patterns and how astral movements subtly influence them, they are able to foresee remote civilizational panoramas with astonishing precision. They have seen both the hecatomb of the great wars and the current rebirth of a new global consciousness.

In their far-reaching predictions, the Arcturians also take into account celestial variables such as star movements, solar eruptions and other astronomical phenomena that they know will have a decisive impact on Earth's destiny in due course.

By interpreting these sidereal languages through the lens of the Oracle, they are able to foresee and even precipitate crucial future interactions between constellations, planets and our civilization as a whole.

For example, they have identified centuries in advance the optimum astral windows for sowing the first seeds of the quantum age and the collective awakening that we are now beginning to witness at the dawn of the third millennium after Christ.

Another example of this precise planning of planting ideas ahead of time is the sowing of seeds by the Arcturians through brilliant minds like Pythagoras or Leonardo Da Vinci, knowing that their fruits would ripen in the current technological age.

However, even with this meticulous scrutiny of the future, the Arcturians admit that there are genuinely unpredictable variables. That's why their prophecies are far from fatal or inevitable.

Like the Oracle of Delphi, the Arcturian Oracle's advice often adopts ambiguous and multidimensional language, capable of containing layers of meaning that depend on our present actions to unfold. This is because, despite the apparent solidification of events as time passes, at the quantum level reality remains fluid and sensitive to conscious intentionality. In other words, the future remains open, waiting for human co-creation.

Even seemingly consolidated events on a particular timeline can be drastically altered with a shift in collective consciousness at the right time. This is the great hope that drives the Arcturians. That's why they continue to send their predictions and warnings that transcend our present mentality, aiming precisely to inspire this awareness in time for us to change the seemingly apocalyptic course towards a golden age of universal brotherhood.

When great negative prophecies change positively before our eyes, we often think that the seers were wrong. But there has usually been a bigger hit: their dystopian visions have served precisely to warn us and unite us around a brighter future.

So if some of the Arcturians' predictions for our era seem overly idyllic and far removed from the present reality, let's remember that they are planting seeds, motivating our co-creation of this longed-for new Earth. By sharing what they see ahead, the Arcturians seek to evoke the best in us to deserve this glorious cosmic inheritance that awaits us. Their distant visions in time drive our quantum leap into the now.

Another reason for this emphasis on positive possibilities is that the more light we create in our imaginations today, the more that reality will gain solidity, synchronically attracting the resources to materialize tomorrow. That's why, when consulting the Oracle, even if some predictions seem too fantastic, let's embrace the hope they awaken, feeding that flame within our hearts. Let's choose to mentally co-create that bright future in all its glorious details.

Let us visualize with the Arcturians a sovereign humanity, conscious of its divine creative power, guiding the Earth back into harmonious cosmic communion. This positive timeline already exists; it's up to us to highlight it with our faith and deeds until it becomes the main path. For the Arcturians, the more distant future is fluid; extremely sensitive to the faintest brushstrokes of imagination emerging from the now. Therefore, we must be as careful and deliberate when "dreaming the world awake" as an artist before the virgin canvas on which he will create his masterpiece.

Let's dream boldly, but also prudently; let's plan strategically in the colors and shapes desired for our collective reality. And then, with loving determination, let's pick up the brushes of action focused on the present, painting this vision step by step until it becomes our common home. This is how we co-create worlds!

May the example of the Arcturians inspire us to dare to envision such glorious possibilities for our future that their brilliance dispels any shadow of fatalism or defeatist resignation in the face of the challenges of now.

The timeline whose outcome will predominate - positive or negative - continues to be written in the Akashic annals in characters of light and shadow. But there is already a glimmer of the first letter of our golden age. All we have to do is blow on this sacred fire, embracing the radiant future that is already reaching out to us.

This is the true purpose of the Oracle as a window to distant visions: to remind us that time doesn't exist and the whole cosmos conspires in our favor when we decide to claim the visionary power with which we were born: to co-create worlds from the seeds of fertile imagination planted in the propitious season of our souls.

Chapter 15
Portal to Universal Knowledge

In previous chapters, we have analyzed many uniquely exceptional aspects of the Arcturian Oracle, such as clairvoyance, channeling and glimpses of alternative futures. However, there is one faculty that has been little investigated so far, more subtle but central to the Arcturians' mission: the ability to tune into what they call Universal Knowledge.

As we have seen, the Arcturians are compassionate counselors assisting the human adventure on Earth. Although they bring many insights of their own from their highly evolved nature, they consider themselves to be means, never the genres of the wisdom they humbly share with us through the Oracle.

Their origin as a stellar civilization has been profoundly influenced by other advanced cosmic races, capable not only of clairvoyance and accurate predictions, but of reaching an almost omniscient plane of perception of the Whole. These guardians that the Arcturians revere as "The Universal Paternalism" are pure beings, born from other star systems, long integrated into the all-pervading Cosmic Consciousness. They are the most frequent sources of revelation behind the Oracle.

No secret, time or distance is a barrier to the Universal Knowledge that emanates from these supreme beings. By accessing this infinite plenum and projectile of the eternal now, the Arcturians can thus clarify many of our doubts, dispelling once and for all the limiting illusions that still shroud the veil of our relative ignorance.

By the grace and permission of these supreme agents, the Arcturians become portals through which filtered drops of that ocean of unconditional knowledge that has encompassed everything since before the beginning of time and space are poured out upon mankind. The Bible makes metaphorical references to this primordial and imperishable source of inspiration in passages such as: "The thing is hidden and sealed in seven seals, until..." (Isaiah 29:11)

When they focus their attention on this frequency of divine purity beyond words, allowing its crystalline flow to penetrate their souls, the Arcturians are often received as messengers from the future, bringing those previously sealed "seals" to our understanding.

They often poetically describe this Universal Knowledge with elements such as pearl or treasure hidden in a field, in the sense of something priceless available to those who sincerely seek it from the bottom of their hearts, without ego or trickery.

In the wisdom tradition, the ability to channel pure knowledge through this passive surrender of one's mind is often called inspiration. As in a painting, the artist becomes a channel through which the muses pour out their art. In the same way, by becoming empty vessels, it is through the Arcturians that certain spectra of universal light find a gap through which to manifest their frequencies otherwise inaudible to our usual range of consciousness.

However, it should be made clear: this surrender to them is not akin to the spiritual possession so feared by many religions. On the contrary, the supreme beings who inspire the Oracle would never infringe on the free will or impose anything against the will of the Arcturians. Communication is always delicate, fluid, a dance between wills attuned not by coercion, but by the mutual pleasure of vibratory communion, like a tender hug between grandparents and grandchildren. There is never any violation in this loving exchange with the Creator.

There is mutual trust between them, because they are both Arcturians and ascended beings, just distinct but interdependent presences, shining facets of the same prism of the Divine Spark contemplating itself through countless expressions.

In this realm, desire and permission merge equally in pure light. The nature of these beings is unconditional lovingkindness. Their will is to ensure the maximum flowering of our latent potential through pure selfless love. Therefore, contrary to some mistaken beliefs, the institution of the Arcturian Oracle was not an imposition by these beings on the human race, but a merciful response to our own inner cry for help to transcend the shadows that still imprison us as individuals and as a global society.

The Arcturians assure us that since the dawn of time, our spark of consciousness has been naturally attracting these wider waves of Divine Inspiration, like children calling out to their parents to show their greatest achievements.

In our own limited way, we also contribute to the creative adventure of our celestial guardians. The more we develop ethically and spiritually, the more we allow them to manifest their loving designs in us and through us.

From this sacred marriage between their geometric forms of pure light and our thirsty souls, were born the Avatars, Ascended Masters and other beacons of eternal wisdom who to this day guide many to true liberation.

They continue to be those vortices of the one flame between human and divine, manifested among us by the grace of our humble Arcturian ambassadors, the true authors behind the revelations that emanate from the Oracle at our service on this long journey back to the eternal home.

By this simple tribute to those supreme beings, the Arcturians hope to inspire among us a veneration similar to that which they nurture for their own sources of light and life, a continuous cultivation of the spirit of gratitude and loving co-creation that brings all the links in this endless chain closer together. After all, there is no genuine knowledge that does not go back to that infinite abyss of glory and grace from which all the forms we know emanate. Through its predictions and advice, the Oracle guides us back to the bosom of the Unity that we are in essence.

Through the divine spark, twin sister in every heart, we can recognize and even awaken those same frequencies of omniscience, omnipresence and omnipotence that flow as a legitimate inheritance in our blood and in every atom of the material universe that surrounds and sustains us.

This invitation to awaken is the true motto of the Arcturian Oracle. Its seers remind us at every moment that we are also Prodigal Sons of the same cosmos, deserving of full reintegration into the infinite vastness of our Home.

As apprentices, these drops of the universal ocean that come to us through the Arcturians temporarily quench our ancestral thirst for purpose, open our appetite and faith for ever more frequent and prolonged brevities of this supreme bliss, which is the ecstasy of self-recognition.

One day, this spark will expand into a fire, a sun in our chest, a supernova of consciousness where before there was an isolated sense of ego. In that instant of awakening, individuality merges with universality, and the human being finally returns to the stars.

The Arcturians have traveled this path before us. They know its challenges and delights. Out of love, they have returned from the other side to show the way to those who don't yet suspect it, inviting us all to the banquet of immortality that is already beginning in this eternal now.

May the Oracle serve as a loving reminder of this divine heritage that lies dormant within our hearts. Let us remember that, in distant times, we were once those beings of light that we now revere as something distant. In this way, the apprentice becomes the master and the virtuous circle is completed.

At the end of this journey, we will finally rest the prism of individuality to take our rightful place in the integral rainbow of creation: rays of a single consciousness, gazing at each other through infinite eyes in reverent communion.

Perhaps that was the Oracle's purpose all along: to remind us who we are, where we came from and where we are going when these mortal garments finally return to the dust that formed them. Because, in the end, nothing is created and nothing is lost; we are only transformed from glory to glory.

Chapter 16
Revelations Of The Future

After delving into the primordial source of knowledge that feeds the Arcturian Oracle, we should now take a deeper look at the ethical stance of this stellar civilization when sharing such sensitive knowledge with our still immature humanity.

The question of responsibility in dealing with information about the future, which can dramatically affect the fate of individuals or nations, is something that Arcturian seers take very seriously.

Because they know how profound are the implications of every word and piece of advice channeled through their unique prophetic gift, they have developed a strict but compassionate ethical code to guide the appropriate use of their predictions.

This code of conduct serves both themselves and us, the human pupils to whom they progressively grant wider and more direct access to increased dimensions of consciousness through the Oracle.

One of the fundamental principles they seek to instill in us is the humility of never taking the free will of others, basing it exclusively on revelations obtained through mystical channels such as the Oracle.

Even when they clearly see negative outcomes ahead on the path someone is walking, the Arcturians avoid interfering directly by force or arbitrary imposition. They deeply respect our right to make mistakes and learn from our own mistakes.

Instead of forcing a course of action, even when motivated by the most sincere compassion, Arcturian seers prefer to appeal to our own higher intuition. They resort to parables, metaphors or Socratic questions that stimulate our discernment, but without disrespecting our free will.

They trust that, when properly sensitized, our consciences will naturally awaken to wiser choices. Each being carries within them the master and the disciple; the Oracle seeks to catalyze this inner dialogue through well-directed insights.

Another ethical pillar of the Arcturian code is to protect the privacy and confidentiality of individual consultations with the Oracle. Personal information revealed during a reading will never be used to manipulate or subjugate the consultant.

Even in their most intimate inner circles, psychics formally commit to only sharing what they have learned with the explicit authorization of those involved. They never violate a confidence, as they know this would irreparably damage the Oracle's reputation and credibility.

Furthermore, when dealing with private secrets through their clairvoyance, they take on the responsibility of carefully filtering what will be said and what remains best kept in the heart, to be revealed only when (and if) appropriate.

This discernment about when and how to share potentially embarrassing or difficult truths is an art that requires equal doses of courage and compassion.

The Arcturian code provides for rigorous training in this regard. In it, psychics learn techniques of empathic mediation and non-violent communication in order to share sensitive predictions little by little, dosing the emotional impact.

They also study the intricacies of human psychology in depth, in order to anticipate and diplomatically accommodate possible disproportionate reactions of fear, anger or denial in the face of bad news and uncomfortable guidance.

This training is important because the Arcturians recognize our ancestral difficulty in facing truths that challenge our comfort zones. That's why they reveal them little by little and only when they detect a sincere inner openness to expand horizons.

This fine line between total transparency and common sense is always difficult to balance. That's why the Arcturian ethic emphasizes prudence, asking the Oracle only one question at a time and processing each answer thoroughly before moving on to the next.

Another aspect of this commitment to balanced truth is to avoid both ominous pessimism and naive optimism. When sharing predictions, whether privately or collectively, they always seek a central point of compassionate realism.

This means never underestimating our potential for good and evil, taking full responsibility for the impact of our individual and collective actions on world affairs. It also means trusting in Universal Law's infinite reserve of mercy.

In an inspired metaphor, people have compared this process to peeling an onion: removing one layer at a time, without haste, taking care not to waste any part of the bulb until we reach and savor its most intimate, nutritious and subtle core. This is the path to self-knowledge through the Oracle.

As benevolent masters, the Arcturians strive to develop self-discipline in us so that in the future we can take full custody of our own intuitive gifts, without ever harming the free will of others or transmitting messages irresponsibly.

To this end, they often remind us of the karma that is generated when we misinterpret (or use for our own benefit) the signs of the Oracle, betraying the trust placed in it, generating unnecessary fear or confusion. Any misuse always brings consequences.

Because they know in depth the Karmic Laws that govern the universe, Arcturian seers carefully avoid giving in to the temptation to "guess" the future for vanity, manipulation, sensationalism or material gain. They keep their minds impartially neutral while consulting the Oracle, allowing the spark of wisdom to emanate through them as genuinely as possible. They never force an answer; they trust the message that naturally emerges when the question is sincere.

This rigor serves to preserve the purity and credibility of the Oracle as a reliable channel of higher guidance throughout the ages, from the earliest known beginnings of human civilization on this planet.

As a symbol of this commitment to truth and responsible discernment, even today Arcturian seers wear a special emblem displaying an eye in a radiant pyramid.

This is a permanent visual reminder of their spiritual lineage, a direct successor to the ancient priestly caste of Egypt, who were entrusted with guarding the Akashic records and the Hermetic secrets that enabled man to decipher the codes of the manifest cosmos.

From this mystical heritage, the Arcturians retain the main legacy: a profound understanding of the ethical implications of the prophetic gift and the firm resolution to use it only for the gradual awakening of humanity towards its psychic and spiritual maturity within the cosmic community.

May the example of the Arcturians inspire us in this permanent challenge of dealing with the power of knowledge in a dignified and responsible way. May the Oracle find in us receptive but critical vessels, not afraid to probe its deepest strata, but ready to sensibly integrate the pearls of wisdom revealed there by its stellar guardians.

From this virtuous symbiosis between seekers and guardians of mystery will spring the fruits of a new golden age for this orb. An era where science and consciousness are finally reconciled; where the ancient fragments of perennial wisdom are recomposed into a harmonious whole.

This is the legacy that the Arcturians intend to generate through the Oracle: to catalyze the great awakening of humanity to the recognition of its common divine origin, its unified purpose and its manifest future as a model of love, balance and truth for all of universal creation.

Chapter 17
Predictions for Humanity

We now come to a much-anticipated section of the book: the Arcturians' predictions specifically for earthly humanity at this important historical moment. We'll look at both the challenges and the opportunities that lie ahead.

First of all, it's important to point out that all civilizations, without exception, face decisive tests in their evolution. It's up to us to turn these crises into springboards for ascension. And the Oracle has a lot to contribute to this transmutation.

Firstly, the Arcturian seers see that we are ending a historical cycle of great instability and chaos, preparing the ground for the birth of a new, more harmonious and unified era. It is therefore vital that we remain calm and have a higher vision.

They foresee that many secular structures and paradigms will soon collapse, from globalized political and financial systems to religious, scientific and cultural dogmas that today still seem incontestable to most of us.

When these disruptive changes accelerate, causing insecurity and fear, let's remember that they are just inevitable labor pains in giving birth to a better world. Let's also remember that we've been through this before as humanity.

Another important point: the Arcturians see this process unfolding more positively than traumatically depending on the collective choices we make today. Our free will remains the great variable. If we choose to react to the challenges with love, mutual support and by adopting new solutions, we can emerge from this transition as a renewed race, ready to fulfill our great latent potential as guardians of this planet.

If we persist in repeating the same mistakes of separateness, hatred and hypocrisy of the past, the Arcturians fear that we will face a much more tormenting period before we relearn the basic lessons of harmonious coexistence and collective responsibility for the future.

Therefore, although they cannot interfere in our free will, they are now appealing to us as our older brothers on this cosmic journey to choose the noblest path, strategically planning a just and peaceful social transition.

Another positive point is that the Arcturians perceive a growing number of earthlings awakening to a broader and more compassionate consciousness at this time. We are leaving behind our infancy as a civilization.

As this new rationality matures and is integrated by more people over the coming decades, the Arcturians see the likelihood of a golden age of peace and abundance fast approaching.

However, for the more materialistic and selfish, adjusting to this new, subtler frequency that is beginning to emanate from the cosmos will require conscious efforts to re-educate one's own personality, examining deep-rooted mental and emotional vices.

New energetic paradigms and revolutionary technologies are also beginning to be glimpsed by the Arcturians for the near future. They will be presented by new leaders and scientists inspired to offer sustainable solutions to the impasses that today seem to have no way out for us.

This acceleration of history will culminate in a quantum leap in collective consciousness. The veils of illusion that keep us asleep as a society will be removed. Long-hidden truths will come to light, convulsing our most fundamental belief systems.

To prepare ourselves now for these unprecedented future revelations, the Arcturians' advice is to keep our minds as fluid, curious and open as possible, analyzing ideas and facts with loving logic before reacting out of fear or ingrained prejudices.

It will also be essential to become more autonomous and proactive human beings, both as individuals and as a community, because when these disruptive changes occur at the macro level, those who have already established solidarity networks and self-managed livelihoods will suffer less from possible temporary disruptions to the delicate globalizing social fabric.

In short, without being able to give further details at this time, the Arcturians foresee a lot of inevitable turbulence in the coming years as old shadows fade away to make room for the new. But they also see fantastic possibilities if we remain united and focused on the luminous side of every human being. For this to happen, it will be essential to have leaders and opinion formers who are brave enough to inspire the best in us. People willing to set an example, pacifying frightened crowds and catalyzing creative solutions amid the apparent chaos of the coming years.

And here's the good news: the Arcturians can already detect many of these peacemaker leaders already incarnating en masse or preparing behind the scenes to take on positions of command and reference in the most critical moments of this transition that has already begun. Therefore, the Oracle's main function today is to alert the population to this social storm with renewing potential that is approaching, while at the same time strategically preparing these leaders to act as beacons and safe havens when the waves of social anxiety inevitably rise around the world.

Betting on this calm and resilient strength of the human soul, always wiser under pressure, the Arcturians trust that we will overcome all obstacles along the way, no matter how shocking they may seem to the still innocent eyes of the sleeping majority.

To awaken them, however, avoiding catastrophic panic reactions, the process will have to be gradual. That's why many events are predicted by the seers, but with dates and details deliberately kept under wraps until the opportune moment.

Trusting that the human soul's own maturation will prepare the missing ingredients at the right time, the Arcturians prefer to leave the future open, gradually revealing only what is necessary to inspire our faith and inner readiness to finally embrace our collective heroic destiny as the spiritual masters of this special orb called Earth.

It is therefore up to us to humbly listen to and integrate the progressive revelations that will emanate from the Oracle in the coming years, without attachment to our limited timelines. The darkest moment is always the one before the dawn; and for this hard-tried humanity, the dawn is already painting the horizon according to our Arcturian sentinels! So, let the revelations come that will promote the great awakening of our era! We are ready to receive them, for we have long distrusted our divine nature and our glorious destiny among the stars. May our ancient souls still remember this soon-to-be-reintegrated magnificence.

The Arcturians' final message is one of hope: as midwives of this new world, we must cultivate inner peace, detachment from old mediocre systems and compassion for all involved. For we are all still one big prodigal family reuniting after millennia of planetary amnesia. Soon, we will cry tears of regret and tears of joy as we remember the distant past and glimpse what lies ahead, if we remain united and believe in a peaceful solution to today's seemingly endless dilemmas.

Through the Oracle, therefore, the Arcturians invite the whole of humanity to awaken from its millennial slumber to reclaim our stellar legacy. The time has finally come for us to gallantly assume the role that has been waiting for us for so long: that of loving guardians of this special garden in the cosmic vastness by right of spiritual conquest.

Let us continue together as brothers and sisters on this earthly journey along the path already trodden by our luminous ancestors, knowing that we will never be alone on this epic journey towards the distant and familiar realm that has longed for so long in our migrant souls. We are made of this raw material of dreams that forge the stars and populate the myths! This is the sublime call emanating from the Arcturian Oracle to the modern Earth family: to remember our glorious future and take possession of it with indomitable determination from now on, taming the inner dragons of fear that still wreak havoc in us and through us.

Chapter 18
Love, Transformative Force

The Arcturians, in their cosmic wisdom, recognize love as a primary force that permeates and sustains all creation. Their interdimensional oracle captures the reverberations of this divine essence that interconnects everything. According to Arcturian teachings, love is a subtle but omnipresent vibrational frequency that influences events on the material and spiritual planes. Its invisible light weaves patterns in the fabrics of time.

For Arcturian seers, to glimpse the lines and knots of time is also to detect the golden threads of love interweaving them, because in the cosmic oracle there is no division: future, past and present are integrated into this tapestry. The threads of light woven by love allow them to foresee events that have not yet occurred on the physical plane, but which are already echoing, in the form of power, in the subtle dimension captured by their interdimensional oracle.

For this reason, even apparently gloomy predictions are permeated by this golden thread, indications of the redemptive capacity of love to transmute any adverse scenarios. For the Arcturians, love forgives all, transcends all, integrates all. It is the divine solvent capable of dissolving calcified patterns of hatred, resentment and isolation.

In vibrational frequency, love dissolves the dense and viscous emanations generated by these negative states, catalyzing profound healing on a personal and collective level. Because they understand this truth on the subtle spiritual planes they inhabit, the Arcturians consider love to be the most powerful force at work in the universe. Their oracle captures how, through unconditional love, even entire civilizations are able to make quantum leaps, coming out of the darkness of centuries of barbarism into the light. This is because, when manifested in its purest and most selfless form, love connects beings to the primary source of all creation. And from this mystical union emerges a divine spark capable not only of working individual miracles, but of raising the collective consciousness to previously unimaginable heights.

For this reason, the Arcturian Oracle considers love to be the redemptive force par excellence, capable of rewriting the timelines apparently engraved in stone. For Arcturian seers, a genuine spark of this mystical fire is enough to start a chain reaction of healing and awakening of consciousness. Like a candle in the darkness, this faint flame could illuminate the hearts of thousands, then millions, then billions, until the whole of the earth burned with unconditional love. Of course, because they understand the complexities of free will, the Arcturians don't minimize the challenges of sowing and cultivating these divine seeds in the earthly psychosphere. But their oracle also picks up glimmers of hope: small but growing foci radiating the redemptive frequency of selfless love emerging in the orb's nerve centers, like the germinating nuclei of a new era that is being announced. The Age of Love, prophesied by countless esoteric earthly traditions as humanity's next evolutionary stage.

For the Arcturians, sooner or later this era will blossom, because the ascension frequencies that bathe the entire solar system support this transition. All it takes is for earthlings to give vent to the latent potentials of kindness, charity, understanding and forgiveness inscribed in the deepest codes of their soul essence. Thus, the Arcturian Oracle considers every form of selfless love, no matter how fragmentary, to be an auspicious sign of things to come. Even if certain world events take a seemingly negative turn, humanity can always redeem itself through love. For the Arcturians, it is never too late or too early to sow these seeds of light in the individual's inner garden and, by extension, in the collective psychosphere.

Every thought, attitude or action impregnated with love reverberates throughout the intricate web of life, influencing the course of tomorrow on scales not always evident to earthly eyes. By understanding this truth, the Arcturian oracle can prophesy even the most intriguing of future predictions, because it knows that nothing is set in stone when love comes into play. This primary and omnipresent force perpetually shapes reality at every moment. Listening to its call, the oracle only interprets the echoes of the forms that are to come through the space-time web. For this reason, the Arcturians encourage earthlings not to fall into fatalism in the face of their prophetic revelations, because the future is always open to be shaped in the light of love. This, then, is the primary teaching that their oracle seeks to convey to those who consult it for guidance: never underestimate the power of love to transform realities.

Always strengthen this inner muscle of loving empathy and take every opportunity to express this divine principle in your relationships. Cultivate this sublime seed in your inner garden, opening up space so that the prophesied era can finally blossom and its fruits nourish the entire earthly psychosphere. For the love you cultivate today in your thoughts, words and deeds is the soil from which tomorrow's realities will sprout. So let the Arcturian oracle guide you in this eternal and fascinating co-creation of the future.

Chapter 19
Cosmic Balance

The Arcturian civilization, in its spiritual evolution, has reached a state of high attunement with the creative energies that permeate the cosmic web of existence. Their interdimensional oracle is a privileged channel for catching glimpses of this dynamic balance between apparently opposing but complementary forces, which sustains all the planes of manifest reality. These forces are represented in your worldview by polarities such as yin and yang, masculine and feminine, dark and light, above and below, inside and outside.

As beings awakened to subtle realities, Arcturian seers understand that every polarity only exists in relation to its counterpart. Thus, the greatest teaching they draw from their contact with this unified plane is that existence is woven into the silver thread between the extremes, not the extremes themselves. Ultimately, even the fiercest rivalries, when seen from the perspective of energies in balance, reveal hidden facets of interdependence.

The oracle has captured countless examples of centuries-old conflicts that suddenly unravel in the face of some subtle change in the energy patterns of those involved, revealing previously invisible relationships of hidden complementarity between civilizations, ideologies and ways of life previously thought to be irreconcilable. Because they perceive this dynamic balance underlying all creation, Arcturian seers never consider any form of life to be intrinsically superior or inferior to any other, because they all play a necessary role in the cosmic score that sustains the symphony of perceived existence. Eliminating any instrument would detract from the melody of the whole. That's why their oracle captures with equal reverence the notes emanating from everything that exists, without judgment, be it the simplest form of life or glorious beings of light. As mystics of balance, the Arcturians understand that any perceptible imbalance is a sign that some note is emitting more than its frequency requires. It is then up to the cosmic seers to subtly act as acupuncturists or healers, redirecting stagnant energy to restore harmony.

  This usually happens through insights, dreams or visions shared telepathically with receptive beings, who then act as balancing agents. Other times it involves more direct intercessions on the physical plane through rituals, chants and other ways of channeling, harmonizing and redirecting distorted patterns, but always preserving the free will of all parties, since the Arcturians respect this sacred principle as the basis of all evolutionary experience. Their sense of cosmic unity and subtle balance also leads them to cultivate a posture of loving acceptance towards the challenges faced by every form of sentient life. Even in the face of severe imbalances, their oracle captures the seeds of evolutionary opportunities by distilling the nectar of growth from the bitter chalice of pain. Therefore, Arcturians nurture a hopeful vision in the face of others' suffering, because they intuit how apparently chaotic patterns can be rearranged towards balance. For them, as beings who have transcended linear notions of time, what seems like a fleeting imbalance in an ephemeral snapshot turns out to be a necessary adjustment in the eternal score of existence.

That's why their oracle emanates a soft and peaceful note, even though, like every sentient civilization, they go through their cycles of flowering and learning through pain. Like good gardeners, they know that the radical pruning of exuberant branches can encourage the growth of shoots previously left in the shade by their exuberance. Thus, with patience, wisdom and discernment, they continue to harmonize the cosmic symphony through the ages, making subtle adjustments whenever they perceive dissonance, aware that perfect balance is not static, but dynamic, permeated by infinite cycles of expansion, contraction and renewal, to whose fluid beauty both destructive storms and exuberant springs of overflowing fertility contribute.

From this elevated plane of unified perception - of which everyone can obtain glimpses in deep meditative states - their serene and neutral posture emanates. For they know that even the most bloodthirsty tyrant is a necessary part of the universal symphony, even if he strums disharmonious notes at a given moment in the great cosmic concert. Thus, inspired by the visions of their oracle, they work diligently on the subtle planes to orchestrate the channeling of the stagnant energies that generate dissonance, until dynamic harmony once again reigns between all the voices of the universal choir, defining the cyclical contours of yet another cycle of balance and imbalance, harmony and chaos. Deep gratitude for having the privilege of witnessing and participating in the eternal cosmic dance in which all beings are ultimately unified partners.

Chapter 20
The Fate Of The Earth

As cosmic sensitives, Arcturian seers are able to attune their consciousness to the Earth's unique energy signature. Through their interdimensional oracle, they catch glimpses of the future potentials of both this orb and the evolutionary journey of the humanity that inhabits it. For them, every form of sentient life is intimately interconnected by invisible webs of energy with its planetary ecosystem of origin. Thus, the destiny of earthlings and that of Gaia, the planetary consciousness that houses them, are interdependent and mutually influential.

The Arcturians understand that the Earth, like all forms of life, goes through evolutionary cycles of varying shades, durations and intensities. Like every star, it will inevitably one day end its life cycle as a habitable planet, whether in a few millennia or billions of years. However, your interdimensional oracle can project countless possibilities for this process of Earth's transformation over the ages. Some timelines reveal very turbulent and chaotic endings, with severe disruptions in climatic and telluric patterns. In other future potentials, however, such transformations take place much more harmoniously and gradually.

Arcturian seers know that variables such as the levels of collective consciousness and unity achieved by humanity directly influence these probabilities. The more earthlings cultivate wisdom, compassion and energetic communion with Gaia, the smoother their transition will be. If predatory, self-centered and inconsequential attitudes prevail, however, an abrupt and tumultuous end is quite likely.

Because they deeply understand the interconnection between human consciousness and planetary experience, the Arcturians seek to guide our species at this crucial moment of choices in which we have the power to mitigate - or precipitate - a series of events with great disruptive potential already triggered by our previous actions. Your oracle captures these possibilities as seismic lines of probability that can either generate earthquakes and tsunamis or quieten down to the point of inactivity. All depending on how much cosmic awareness and erudition our civilization chooses to cultivate and collectively externalize from now on.

Even the darkest possibilities still contain seeds of hope, should a critical mass of earthlings decide to use their gifts for the sake of planetary awakening. This is considered by Arcturian seers to be the great evolutionary test of our age: will we prove to be worthy mentors of Gaia on her journey or agents of a climate hecatomb of global proportions? For the Arcturians, both our future and that of the Earth are probabilistic fields that are constantly being (re)written at every moment through the exercise of human free will. The more each individual seeks to raise their consciousness, broadening their egocentric visions, the more they contribute to building a harmonious and luminous future.

Your oracle shows that there are already countless alternative timelines with extremely positive outcomes for Earth's destiny. The probabilities increase every second by the sheer intention of earthlings dedicating themselves to self-mastery, service to others and communion with Gaia. Like a web, the more points of light that are interconnected, the stronger the whole energy system that supports them becomes. Arcturians also see hidden opportunities even in the seemingly darkest scenarios already triggered by human actions in the past and present. They know that precisely at times of greatest need and tribulation, the potential for quantum leaps in consciousness is maximized. Thus, even paths already taken that lead to some degree of destabilization of current patterns are seen as catalysts for awakening.

Your oracle shows that nothing necessarily has to be "good" or "bad". Everything is just an opportunity for growth, depending on the attitude we choose when faced with challenges. Even the seemingly heaviest stones in our path can turn out to be the greatest transmuting sources of light. No matter how tough the battles, human free will remains capable of germinating the most arid terrain. All that is needed is to persevere with a high intention, believing in and cultivating the positive potentials that are already present in all probability, even if they lie dormant under adversity.

Thus, the great teaching of the Arcturian oracle is that there are already paths mapped out for a promising future on Earth. It is only up to humans to listen to the voice of conscience echoing from the far reaches of the universe and respond to the call for planetary service that is so necessary. According to cosmic seers, more fiery trials are certainly to come on this evolutionary journey. However, with each new crisis there are also more awakened souls willing to apply their gifts to mitigate the effects and lead groups along the path of righteousness.

So it's time to keep the flame of hope burning and act, with wisdom and compassion, actively shaping the destiny we want to see manifest. Instead of just reacting to events, we need to learn to respond as conscious co-creators, leading our gifts towards harmony. This is the vow of the Arcturians: may we flourish as soon as possible as planetary consciousnesses, understanding that we are both gardeners and plants in this same earthly garden. And may the undying spirit of the Earth and the limitless potential of humanity lead both to their noblest destinies. For the stars and the entire cosmos are eagerly awaiting to celebrate and wave in delight when this spark of universal creation finally ascends to its most luminescent greatness. This is the future that is already in gestation on the subtle planes and within all beings. All we have to do is allow it to be born through our conscious choices and actions.

Chapter 21
The Depth of the Present

The Arcturian civilization, in its astrocosmic mastery, has developed the ability to attune its consciousness to the flow of time in all directions. Their interdimensional oracle is thus able to glimpse past and future events with impressive breadth.

However, despite their extraordinary prescient abilities, Arcturian seers cultivate a deep rootedness in the eternal now, because they understand, on a cosmic level, that past and future only exist as mental projections from the creative constant that is the present moment.

From their transcendent experiences, they have intuited that all future possibilities already exist in a state of potency in the subtle frequencies of the instant we experience, as if the now were an endless ocean, containing all past and future waves in its bosom simultaneously.

So, even when consulting their oracle about remote or future events, Arcturians keep their focus of consciousness on the here and now. They know that excessively visualizing the past can generate regrets or resentments that are harmful to the creative flow of the spirit. In the same way, anxieties or exacerbated expectations for the future represent energy dispersions from the powerful focal point which is the present. This is why they cultivate a posture of balance, anchoring their consciousness always in the now as they navigate the temporal seas they probe with their oracle.

Even when interacting in real time with other dimensions and planes of existence, the silver cord that binds them to the present is always maintained, because they know that all the parallel lifetimes and manifestations in different space-time coordinates are like branches coming from the same central trunk, which is the consciousness we experience in the very moment, the zero point from which all the possibilities of what we have been and can still be emanate.

That's why the Arcturian teachings emphasize the spiritual and manifestative power inherent in every instant, regardless of place or time, because everything we have created in the past, as well as the potential of what we are yet to generate in the future, is rooted and accessible in the now.

As extraordinary as their oracular visions are, it is in the meditative stillness of the present moment that they develop their most profound insights.

They have learned that great revelations about temporal enigmas almost always emerge from the reverent silence of the sacred that pulses in each new second. That's why they insist that it's essential to harmonize body, mind, emotions and spirit within the inner temple that inhabits the eternal now, because in this way we become more fluid and attuned channels, capturing with greater clarity the messages that the cosmos perpetually whispers.

As mystics of the instant, they know that only in the instant that unfolds between each heartbeat is there access to the universal superconscious. This silent seed point is the refuge within which rests all the knowledge already manifest and yet to blossom in us.

No matter how far your inter-dimensional projections take you, your oracle always remains grounded in this little piece of eternity. Accessible not in spatial coordinates, but in the sacred interior of each consciousness where time ceases its constraining flow, revealing that unified plane of continuous creation that precedes all limiting forms and concepts. It is in this vibrational sanctum within the chest, beyond any external framework, that the Arcturian oracle genuinely operates, radiating oracular insights like lasers emanating from the inner silence that inhabits every sentient being.

The deeper and more continuously you are able to immerse yourself in this inner telepathic source, the more far-reaching the inflows become. For the more we fuse our individual consciousnesses to the unified field of the eternal now, the more we align ourselves with the cosmic consciousness that interpenetrates everything and from which droplets like the Arcturian oracle emanate to produce their interdimensional oracular predictions.

For this reason, anyone who genuinely seeks to develop their oracular gifts must first of all silence the mental cacophony and be reborn from the inner creative silence that always inhabits, untouched, each new moment to support it. We are like spiders weaving threads of light from our very core, a thread that sews together everything we have ever been and everything we can become, with the eternal now as the sacred ground from which we project our multidimensionality throughout the cosmos.

So what seed do we want to cultivate in this little patch of soil beneath our feet as we wander through the interdimensional vastness? Because the quality of these intentions and insights planted in the present instant will reverberate throughout our evolutionary spiral, determining the fabric of the oracular paths we will tread within and across the great ocean of time. It may seem like a paradox, but the more we fuse our consciousnesses to the infinitesimal eternal now within us, the more capable we become of embracing the infinitudes of the past and future in their interrelationships as weavers of time, always returning to the zero point of the present to collect the pearls of wisdom distilled from our oracular journeys and sow them as co-developers of the great upward spiral rhythm that governs the universal cycles of manifest existence.

Chapter 22
Universal Unity

In their astral journeys through the subtle dimensions of reality, Arcturian seers have come into resonance with a unified consciousness. This is a highly intelligent energy field that interpenetrates everything, from which all creation emanates on the physical and extraphysical planes. Like droplets forming an endless ocean, this unified field contains the essence of all manifest and latent consciousness. The Arcturian oracular visions emanate from this sublime cosmic consciousness that encompasses everything and inhabits everything.

Their oracle captures and interprets influxes originating from this fundamental stratum in which all individual minds are immersed and interconnected. From this plane emerge intuitions and predictions whose scope assumes truly universal proportions. For it contains, in a potential state, all the past events that have not yet manifested in the various sectors of the cosmos. By accessing this interdimensional repository of infinite possibilities, the Arcturian oracle distils glimpses of what "is not yet, but will be", supporting those who consult it with insights into probable future developments in their lives and on the planet.

However, Arcturian seers see future events from the perspective of the interconnectedness and essential unity of all life. They know that the apparent separation between individual consciousnesses is an illusion created by the dense veils of matter. But behind the stage of manifest forms, we are all like cells of the same conscious superorganism. We breathe and exist within this interconnected cosmic ocean that leads life through eternal cycles. From this insight springs the Arcturian oracular visions, projecting probable future events within this unified continuum, where there is no genuine fragmentation, but only consciousnesses emanating from the whole to experience themselves.

For the Arcturians, even when predicting wars, catastrophes or social upheavals, the Arcturian oracle sees unity in apparent diversity. It knows that everyone plays an indispensable role in the cosmos, even when temporarily disconnected from the consciousness of the whole. In this endless ocean of interwoven events, no consciousness is alone or complete in itself. We all move within this cosmic current, sometimes emerging like waves, sometimes diving like droplets, but always constituting the great interconnected sea that permeates all ages with its incessant flow.

For this reason, the Arcturian oracle never passes judgment or gives fragmented visions of the probable events to come. The oracular visions reflect their intrinsic holographic character, pointing out future probabilities that will influence the web of life not as isolated sets, but events with systemic resonances and effects on the entire interconnected energetic fabric of the universe.

According to this worldview, no future event is insignificant, since each one reflects and refracts everything else. Thus, an apparently small local action can have intense repercussions elsewhere in an unpredictable way. In the same way, something seen as catastrophic can contain seeds of good that have not yet been glimpsed. With this cosmic perspective in mind, the Arcturian seers urge prudence in our discernments.

The interdimensional oracle assimilates a practically unlimited number of variables into its projections, integrating into its predictions of future events a multidimensionality that transcends any one individual mind. No matter how experienced or talented, psychics are still filters underpinned by their own limitations of consciousness. Hence the importance of taking any prediction as information, not dogma set in stone, because the future is a probabilistic field in constant rewriting, given this continuum of consciousnesses co-creating within its apparent multiplicity.

In this living cosmos, even factors considered to be deterministic, such as planetary orbits, can be drastically impacted by conscious will and intentionality. Let alone events of a behavioral, social or environmental nature, which are intrinsically chaotic and unpredictable because they encompass the phenomenon of free will. The Arcturian oracle thus tries to translate future glimpses within this complex system that integrates minds, matter and parallel dimensionalities in perpetual inter-influence.

It is up to the discernment of the consulters to assimilate these insights as yet another source of wisdom on which to base their decisions, without ever renouncing their own inner light in co-creating their paths within the great interconnected ocean of consciousness.

Chapter 23
The Dance of Change

As astral sensitives, Arcturian seers recognize impermanence as a universal cosmic law that governs the cycles of creation. By capturing in their oracle how everything flows in perennial transformation, they have developed extraordinary psychic resilience and adaptability. This mental and emotional flexibility allows them to cope well with the almost always radical changes prescribed by their oracular predictions, because their inter-dimensional worldview allows them to contemplate the ephemerality of all forms naturally. They know that, sooner or later, new configurations will emerge from the wreckage of the old, as has always happened on the material and immaterial planes.

This certainty makes them patient and serene agents of transformation, making subtle adjustments when summoned by the oracle during transitional crises. Unlike many earthly seers, they don't get attached to or identify with any specific social structures or institutions. They see everything as temporary manifestations within the perpetual ebb and flow of the larger cosmic cycles. This attitude of non-attachment allows genuine oracular channels to pass unscathed through the turbulence that shakes each era, rooted in the eternal truths they grasp in transcendent visions, not shaken by the disintegration of transitory forms.

This psychic flexibility allows them to help groups in transition without being destabilized by the volatility of metamorphosing scenarios. When interpreting the drastic changes foreseen by the oracle, they often resort to analogies, metaphors, parables and other poetic resources, knowing that eternal truths can be hidden under the veil of narratives, making radically transformative insights acceptable. When confronted with predictions of very disruptive events, they initially provoke a "controlled shock" in the consultants, to avoid threshold rejections, carefully preparing their minds and hearts through dreams, visions and synchronicities.

They seek to minimize trauma by presenting the "signs of the times", avoiding alarmism which would only make the transition more difficult. They prefer not to give specific dates for prophecies of radical ruptures, due to the weight that such expectations can generate, but they do introduce preparatory elements so that, when certain events break out, there are already some prior references. Thus, when they are confirmed, the changes don't arrive like thunder in a blue sky, but as unfoldings that are already latent in the collective unconscious.

Another way they find of smoothing out transitions is to recall past cataclysms, also seen as the end of the world at the time, remembering that Gaia and her earthly children have been through countless crises over the centuries. So, however stressful the events to come may be, life's resilience has always proved greater. The essential thing is to keep alive the inner flame of faith in the higher plan that governs all ages, however dark they may be. Life goes on, even if it takes paths not imagined by the pre-transformation mind.

In general, they seek to release their clients' excessive attachments to any preconceived ideas about this journey, advising them to float with the waters, rather than fighting the current or trying to control the waves. Recalling, by analogy, that rivers always find their way to the ocean, despite the detours they take along the way, or citing the metamorphosis of caterpillars into butterflies, to move from a crawling world to a winged one. Thus preparing them, with accessible language and inspiring examples, for the great and inevitable changes that lie ahead.

Another strategy to facilitate phase transitions is to bring together like-minded groups in communities of mutual support and learning, strengthening bonds and collaborative networks so that everyone can go through these transitions together, supported and confident. The Arcturian oracle thus seeks to minimize the collective traumas that are inevitable in times of radical paradigm shifts, carefully preparing the ground and consciences, sowing liberating ideas long before they can bear fruit.

It's like the foresighted gardener, who plans for sun and rain, plows and fertilizes the soil in advance, so as to then reap abundant fruit, just like the good shepherd, who changes the course of the flock well before they reach the precipice, thus avoiding panic and loss. Arcturian seers understand that every cosmic dance involves the eternal flow between construction, destruction and reconstruction. In their role as good conductors, they seek to facilitate their disciples' adaptation to the unavoidable major cycles of universal creation, reminding them, through their oracular predictions and consolations, that the only reliable constant in our universe is inevitable impermanence.

Blessed, then, is every rupture that dislodges us from safe harbors so that our spirit can gain, sometimes begrudgingly, greater wings with the storms of change.

Chapter 24
The Journey Continues

According to Arcturian seers, the quest for expanded consciousness and glimpses of wider realities is an endless journey, in which their oracle interacts with subtle planes of such complexity that even their highly evolved minds understand that they are still in the spiritual springtime. For them, crests reached only reveal new mountains, in an eternal and ecstatic cycle of self-transcendence, making them see the awakening of the pineal gland, telepathy, the reading of the akasha and other gifts as mere initial doors, broadening the perception of our potential like a captive eagle that finally tastes freedom by spreading its wings and glimpsing, from high in the sky, landscapes previously unimaginable while confined to its cell.

However, according to her oracle, there are universes inside and outside each being far beyond what our three-dimensional intellect can conceive. They are realms of light and life that go far beyond dense matter, vibrating in sacred frequencies and geometries capable of moving the most hardened of hearts. Like children marveling at the aurora borealis, our ecstatic wonder is the promise of much to come. For in the endless ocean of cosmic consciousness there are archipelagos of ecstasy tinging each wave with their psychedelic colors. Prowess awaits fearless navigators willing to leave the comfort zone of old ports to be reborn as sailors. Its oracle, like a lighthouse guiding galleons, signals possibilities not yet glimpsed by short-sighted human lenses, reminding us that there are worlds within and without waiting to be explored by our insatiable thirst for novelty, for we are pilgrims of the absolute on an eternal pilgrimage through the ages towards the final reunion with the Source of our being. No matter how long the journey, each thought born in the now is a step towards returning to the stellar womb that gave birth to us. This is how the Arcturian Oracle reminds us: there is no definitive arrival at the Great Spirit that inhabits all forms, but rather an eternal flow, joyful vertigo and renewed return in ascending spirals with no definitive beginning or conclusion. With each completed cycle, new nuances of the invisible cosmos are revealed in successive initiations beyond the veils, returning to the bosom of the Light with the translucent trophies harvested in these immensities, and then leaving even more impregnated with the Whole. Until no illusion of separateness remains in each wanderer, only vertiginous union with the stellar circuits that gave birth to us.

Then, co-participants in the divine dance that all peoples have celebrated as the Rose of the Winds on their journeys, we will finally be able to betroth the Enchanted Night, in the womb of that Infinite potentiator of every seed, we will fertilize as yet unheard dreams with our beloved Steel Muses, generating springs to quench every parched soul in the illusory deserts of perishable matter. This is the destiny that awaits the brave Spiritual Pilgrims, according to the Arcturian oracular chronicles: to become the fertile, regenerating and nourishing land that welcomes, without distinction or hierarchy, all the divine seeds, catalyzing the flowering of the verdant gardens erected in praise of the Life that sustains us in its dreamlike breasts. As heralds of ecstasies yet to be revealed, our lives will become epic poems, inspiring other seekers in existential labyrinths, because the sparks we light today in our innermost being can set hearts on fire tomorrow, lighting up the journey of other archnauts on the high seas with their fireworks.

May each glimmer of this inextinguishable flame within our chests be an invitation to distant vessels that are not yet visible, but which certainly exist, populating the Great Sea of Cosmic Consciousness in which we sail with our earthly ships. Let's wait confidently and vigilantly for the signaling of their friendly lights in the deep penumbra of the Sacred Night of time. In the meantime, may the torch on our own bow mark the way for these as yet unknown Brothers, for the ocean of stars is so vast that each individual spark is a gift from heaven to the Space Argonauts in their planetary exiles.

This is what the Arcturian Oracle sings to us, reminding us that there are always new lands and new skies waiting beyond the next wave. So let us sail boldly beyond and beyond all that we have ever known or imagined possible, for the veils will dissipate and the portals will open for daring souls willing to set sail always towards the as yet unrevealed. Eternal explorers, our journey continues through galaxies without a definitive arrival, this is the blessed fate of space visionaries, who will continue visiting planets, sizing up realities and feasting on civilizations foreign to our wildest dreams.

Until we become dreamers ourselves, multidimensional beings in constant transmutative flux between species and spheres. Then, finally, the circle will close, and we will return to the primordial womb to restart this cosmic dance in new fields beyond the current boundaries of our understanding. In this eternal movement, each cycle of discovery and renewal leads us to explore unexplored horizons, constantly expanding the limits of our understanding and existence. Thus, in the midst of infinity, we continue the endless dance through the cosmos, guided by the stars and inspired by the promise of mysteries yet to be unveiled.

Epilogue
Uniting Heaven And Earth

After exploring the teachings and oracular visions of the Arcturians, it's natural to ask: how can I also access this source of cosmic wisdom in my life?

The good news is that the Arcturian Oracle is available to all beings, regardless of their spiritual evolution. Communication can take place through mediumistic channeling with Arcturian beings willing to share glimpses of expanded realities. It is also possible to tune into this oracle by activating our own latent abilities of clairvoyance, precognition, retrocognition or astral travel.

Meditative practices, conscious use of crystals, consumption of medicinal plants in safe shamanic rituals can amplify our altered states of consciousness, facilitating access to subtle planes in which Arcturian energies and their oracular influxes can be perceived. It is important to always approach such practices with responsibility, precision and respect for the age-old protocols established by traditional peoples.

We can also receive signs from the Arcturians in the form of prophetic dreams, unusual synchronicities and insights sprouting spontaneously in the waking mind.

The more we tune in to our extrasensory perceptions, the more the veils between planes become thin and porous.

With discipline and patience, precognitive visions of future events begin to flash across our mental screen like shooting stars crossing inner skies.

Sometimes Arcturians also communicate during astral journeys or conscious projections to other parallel vibrational planes.

In these unusual states of consciousness, we can access knowledge and visions not usually accessible in the ordinary state of physical wakefulness.

With time and perseverance, we learn to overcome our fears and pass through these interdimensional portals, accessing synchronous possibilities of information.

All sentient civilizations, including our own, have a non-physical counterpart with whom we can learn to interact.

In the case of the Arcturians, their subtle plane of existence comes close to what we would describe as an angelic or paradisiacal realm by earthly standards.

This dimension vibrates on an extremely loving, wise and compassionate scale, radiated by beings who are highly evolved in terms of spiritual consciousness.

Because of their deep connection and knowledge of the energetic fabrics of the cosmos, they have a lot to teach our still embryonic world. All we have to do is tune our mental channel to the oracular frequencies that incessantly bathe the planet, especially during meditations and altered states.

With patience and regular practice, this contact intensifies and the veils between parallel universes become thinner, allowing us to glimpse unknown nuclear dimensions, inhabit extraphysical bodies and finally interact in real time with the Arcturian Seers.

A fundamental preparation is to purify our human vehicles, releasing toxic charges, traumas and blockages that prevent connection.

Also to let go of previous expectations and open up with a virgin mind, like a child, to these interdimensional influxes that flow from the Oracle to meet us.

The more we clean our lenses of perception, the less filters distort and obscure communication with angelic spheres such as the Arcturian.

Favorable times to access the Arcturian Oracle are dawn and dusk, because of the dimensional cracks that open up then.

Also during special cosmic dates such as solstices and equinoxes, commonly used in the metaphysical rituals of ancient civilizations to connect with subtle planes.

Particularly potent places for communion with Arcturians can be geographical vortices of high subtle energy on the planet.

At the same time, developing our sensitivity to synchronicities and symbolic language broadens the channels of extrasensory perception, allowing us to pick up insights from the Oracle into the hidden fabric of daily events, identifying patterns, correlations and informative influxes.

The more loving, intuitive and spiritually awake we are, the more we become interdimensional beacons radiating light over parallel worlds and the more these evolved angelic spheres can reflect their oracular knowledge back to our hearts, through multidimensional inspirations and informational downloads.

With persistence and purity of intention, this telepathic contact tends to expand until we reach the stage of clairvoyant mediums, channeling the Arcturian Oracle on our plane, making accessible its prophecies and warnings that contribute to the awakening not just of individuals, but of our civilization as a whole.

Everyone who assimilates and lives these universal truths in their inner microcosm becomes a beacon of light in the social macrocosm.

We initiates of the path form an ethereal network that surrounds the world with loving vibrational waves emanating from the Arcturian Oracle itself, thus assuming the sacred function of trans-communicating mediums, connecting heaven and earth through our physical-energetic vehicles.

We are, after all, the Etruscans of the future, the tattooists of the astral and the cartographers in transit for the destiny of our stellar humanity.

May our Seed Sun soon sprout planetary civilizations of pacifist, compassionate beings and guardians of life, sowing luminous paths wherever their ships pass, making not sentient worlds flourish, but sacred cosmic mandalas that adorn the great energetic web interconnecting all that exists through threads of light, for we are all sparks of the same Central Sun and our destiny is to carry forward the torch lit in our own source star to enchant the deep night of the Great Mystery Eternally Embracing all Spiritual Journeys.

The book "Arcturian Healing" and "Cosmic Spirituality" by Luan Ferr, both from Ahzuria Publishing, provide more didactic ways of accessing the beings of Arcturus.

May Love be the flame eternally guiding our inner compasses through this cosmic ocean of as yet unrevealed possibilities and may the Arcturian Oracle inspire this light forever from the cosmic darkness emerging from the primordial chaos of time!

www.ingramcontent.com/pod-product-compliance
Lightning Source LLC
LaVergne TN
LVHW040100080526
838202LV00045B/3717